The
Lewis & Clark
COOKBOOK

With Contemporary Recipes

Terri Evenson

Laurie Armstrong

Host Fest
10-2001

Whisper'n
WATERS

ISBN 0-9701378-0-X
Copyright 2000 © by Whisper'n Waters, Inc.
Second Printing December 2000

Authors: Teri Evenson, Lauren Lesmeister and Jeffrey W. Evenson
Design Director: Chelly Bosch, Elegant Designs, Bismarck ND
Recipe Editor: Lauren Lesmeister
Printer: Kromar Printing, Winnipeg, Canada
Publishers: Whisper'n Waters, Inc., Bismarck, North Dakota

Front Cover: "Captain William Clark of the Lewis and Clark Expedition Meeting with the Indians of the Northwest" Charles M. Russell, 1897, oil on canvas. Courtesy of the Sid Richardson Collection of Western Art, 309 Main Street, Fort Worth Texas 76102.
Please Note: Here Clark was meeting the Mandan Indians. The painting depicts tepees rather than earth lodges in which the Mandan lived. Also some items were not used in that era but later on in Charlie Russell's era; like the capote, cradleboard, and clothing styles.

Back of Front Cover: "Meriwether Lewis" by Charles Wilson Peale, oil on wood panel, 1807. "William Clark" by Charles Wilson Peale, Oil on paper, 1810. Courtesy of the Independence National Historical Park Collection, National Park Service.

Back Cover: 1961.195 Charles M. Russell "Lewis and Clark on the Lower Columbia," Watercolor, gouache and graphite on paper, 1905. Courtesy Amon Carter Museum, Fort Worth, Texas.

Front of Back Cover: John F. Clymer, "Sacajawea at the Big Water," oil, 24 X 48 inches 1974. Courtesy of Mrs. Clymer and the Clymer Museum of Art, Ellensburg, Washington.

Dedications

In loving memory of my mother...

I couldn't believe you'd ever leave me and I was right. I heard you in the pines outside my window...and from time to time as I wrote and tested... Thanks for letting me know you're there! Yes, now I'll spend more time with the kids... pretty brown Cathy with the unrestrained laugh... our knight in shining armor Sir Christopher. You were right about husband Jeff. He's a good man. Without him this book would not be possible.

I love you and miss you like everything.

Love, Teri

For Mom, Dad and Jacqueline. Rest easy. Wheel turning.

L.L.

Dedicated to the Drifter's Spirit and the Dreamer's Soul. But most of all, to my loving family and friends, whom empowered me to do both.

Jeff Evenson

Table of Contents

Acknowledgements for Internal Art Works............5

Introduction 6

Soups 9

Appetizers...21

Biscuits, Breads and Dumplings 39

Beans, Salads and Vegetables 57

Buffalo..75

Elk and Venison 93

Fish and Fowl...111

Marinades and Sauces 129

Desserts...147

Assemblage...165

Index...181

Order Forms 185

Acknowledgements for Internal Art Works and Quotes

The following works of Karl Bodmer are courtesy of Joslyn Art Museum, Omaha, Nebraska; Gift of Enron Art Foundation.

Page	Plate	Name
7	164	*Omaha Boy,* watercolor on paper, 10 7/8 X 7 7/8
8	192	*Chan-Chä-Uiá-Teüin, Teton Sioux Woman,* watercolor and pencil on paper, 17 X 11 7/8
19	157	*The Missouri below the Mouth of the Platte,* watercolor on paper, 8 3/4 X 10 3/4
20	151	*Nodaway Island,* watercolor on paper, 8 3/4 X 10 3/4
37	185	*Sioux Camp,* watercolor on paper, 7 1/2 X 10 1/8
38	309	*Mähchsi-Karéhde, Mandan Man,* watercolor and pencil on paper, 16 7/8 X 12
55	182	*Bijoux Hills on the Missouri,* watercolor and pencil on paper, 9 5/8 X 12 1/3
56	257	*Kiäsax, Piegan Blackfeet Man,* watercolor on paper, 12 1/4 X 9 1/2
73	300	*Interior of a Mandan Earth Lodge,* watercolor and ink on paper, 11 1/4 X 16 7/8
74	209	*Landscape with Herd of Buffalo on the Upper Missouri,* watercolor on paper, 9 5/8 X 12 3/8
91	316	*Síh-Chilä, Mandan Man,* watercolor on paper, 17 1/8 X 11 7/8
92	205	*Blackfoot-Assiniboin Girl,* watercolor on paper, 10 5/8 X 8
109	195	*Junction of the Yellowstone and the Missouri,* watercolor on paper, 10 3/8 X 16 3/4
110	270	*View of the Bear Paw Mountains from Fort McKenzie,* watercolor on paper, 11 1/2 X 16 3/8
127	272	*Buffalo and Elk on the Upper Missouri,* watercolor on paper, 9 3/4 X 12 1/4
145	235	*View of Stone Walls,* watercolors on paper, 9 7/8 X 16 7/8
146	221	*Rock Formations on the Upper Missouri,* watercolor on paper, 12 1/2 X 7 3/4
164	260	*Makúie-Póka, Piegan Blackfeet Man,* watercolor on paper, 12 1/4 X 9 7/8

John Clymer's Works Courtesy of Mrs. John Clymer and the Clymer Museum of Art, Ellensburg, Washington.

128	*Salt Makers,* oil, 24 X 48 inches	1975
163	*The Lewis Crossing,* oil, 24 X 40 inches	1968

The Historical Quotes

Quotes courtesy of University of Nebraska Press, taken directly from the "Journals of the Lewis and Clark Expedition, volumes 1-12" edited by Gary Moulton. Published by the University of Nebraska Press. *The Journals of the Lewis and Clark Expedition* are available from the University of Nebraska Press at 800.526.2617 and on the web at nebraskapress.unl.edu.

Quotes from the original Lewis and Clark Journals courtesy of the American Philosophical Society, Philadelphia Pennsylvania.

Quotes from the original Joseph Whitehouse's Journals courtesy of Edward E. Ayer Collection, the Newberry Library, Chicago Illinois.

Introduction

It is in the spirit of discovery that we write this book. Although cooking techniques and people's tastes have changed, we still utilize many of the wild ingredients that Lewis and Clark were so fond of. Our society has evolved to once again embrace roots, leaves and fruits as a staple in our diet as Sacagawea did 200 years ago. Today our diets are enriched with diverse and affordable spices because of our commerce system. Oh, that they could see us now!

The Corps of Discovery has taught us to explore the new, to improve upon what is and to not be wasteful. In that tradition, we have compiled this collection of recipes with many familiar flavors, yet as diverse as the original Corps. We did not restrict our recipes to the ingredients and methods of the Corps but embellished them with today's flavors and styles.

Journey with us now to the sights, impressions and tastes that await your adventuresome spirit. Explore the flavors and the dishes we have journaled on our trip down the trail of discovery.

Teri Evenson

164. *Omaha Boy,* watercolor on paper, 10 7/8 X 7 7/8

192. *Chan-Chä-Uiá-Teüin, Teton Sioux Woman,*
watercolor and pencil on paper, 17 X 11 $^{7}/_{8}$

Soups

In mid-April, Lewis set off to the east. He stopped first in Frederickstown, where on April 15 he wrote General William Irvin, superintendent of military stores, with headquarters in Philadelphia. Lewis said he wanted Irvin to purchase for him some necessary articles. First on the list was "Portable-Soup," a dried soup of various beans and vegetables that Lewis may have used during his travels as an army paymaster. In any case, he was enthusiastic about it. He told Irvin, "Portable Soup, in my opinion, forms one of the most essential articles in the preparation {for the expedition}, and fearing that it cannot be procured readily in such quantity as is requisite, I .....take the liberty to request that you will procure two hundred pounds of it for me," or however much was available on the market. "I have supposed that the soup would cost about one dollar pr lb; should it however, come much higher then quantity must be limited by the sum of $250 as more cannot be expended." In the end, Lewis spent $289.50 on 193 pounds of portable soup, by far the highest sum for any area of provisions. He spent as much for dried soup as he had originally estimated for his instruments, arms, and ammunition.

From "Undaunted Courage" by Stephen E. Ambrose, page 86.

Venison and Smoked Sausage Soup

1 Tablespoon olive oil

1 pound country style smoked sausage, chopped

1 pound venison round steak, 1-inch cubes (or substitute beef)

4 cloves garlic, minced

2 medium onions, large dice

2 stalks of celery, cut on the diagonal

2 Tablespoons of butter

1 teaspoon salt

1 quart tomato juice

2 bay leaves

2 cups of black turtle beans, cooked and drained

6 cups of water

1 small jalapeno pepper, seeded and chopped

1 Tablespoon ground cumin

1 Tablespoon chili powder

1/2 teaspoon freshly ground black pepper

1 Tablespoon fresh oregano, minced

Add oil, sausage and venison to a large cast iron skillet over medium high heat. Quickly stir fry sausage and venison. Place sausage and venison in colander and wash under very hot water to remove excess fat. Set aside. In a clean skillet; sauté garlic, onions and celery in butter until onions are translucent. Add salt, stir, and set aside. In a soup pot, combine tomato juice, bay leaves, beans and water. Bring to a boil, stirring occasionally. Reduce heat and simmer for 10 minutes. Add the meat mixture, vegetable mixture and remaining ingredients. Simmer, stirring occasionally for 20 minutes. Remove from heat, cover and allow flavors to blend at least 30 minutes.

Garnish with sour cream and hot pepper sauce to taste.

Serves 6-8

Elk Meatball Soup

1 1/2 pounds ground elk (substitute venison, buffalo or lean ground beef)

1 egg, beaten

1/4 cup maple syrup

1/2 cup crushed croutons

1/2 teaspoon seasoned salt

1/2 teaspoon fresh ground black pepper

1/4 cup Parmesan cheese, grated

1/2 teaspoon celery seed

6 cups of water

3 sticks beef jerky, cut into matchsticks

1 cup carrots, sliced

1 cup zucchini, large chunks

1 cup onions, chopped

1 cup celery, sliced on the diagonal

1/2 cup rice, precooked

2 bay leaves

1 twenty-eight-ounce can of diced tomatoes, including juice

6 ounces of tomato puree

Combine ground meat, egg, and maple syrup in a mixing bowl. Knead thoroughly. In a large bowl, mix crushed croutons, salt, pepper, Parmesan cheese and celery seed. Blend meat mixture and dry mixture together. Using a melon ball cutter, shape meatballs and let stand on wax paper at room temperature for 25 minutes. Coat a broiler pan with non-stick cooking spray. Place meatballs on broiler pan, 1/2-inch apart. Broil for about 15 minutes or until done. Set aside. Combine remaining ingredients in a large soup pot and bring to a boil. Reduce heat, cover and simmer for 30 minutes, stirring occasionally. Add meatballs and simmer another 30 minutes or until vegetables are tender.

Garnish with additional grated Parmesan cheese.

Serves 10-12

Cornish Game Hens and Butternut Squash Soup

2 Cornish game hens

Dash of salt and pepper

2 cups of butternut squash, cooked

2 cups heavy cream

2 Tablespoons butter

1 clove garlic, minced

1 cup chopped onions

2 Tablespoons fresh scallions, cut fine

1/4 teaspoon dried thyme

6 cups hot chicken broth

2 cups cubed, peeled cantaloupe

1 can (sixteen-ounces) solid-pack pumpkin

diced scallions

paprika

Preheat heat oven to 350 degrees F. Salt and pepper hens inside and out. Place in baking dish. Bake hens uncovered until done. Allow to cool. Debone and tear meat into bite size pieces and set aside. Using a heavy saucepan, heat cream until it begins to bubble. Stir frequently with a whisk until cream is reduced by half (about 45 minutes). Set cream aside. In a large soup pot, sauté garlic and butter for about 3 minutes. Add cooked squash, onions, scallions and thyme. Cook over medium heat for 10 minutes, stirring frequently to prevent sticking. Add small amounts of water if needed. Stir in hot broth, then add cantaloupe and pumpkin. Simmer for 30 minutes, stirring occasionally. Allow to cool to room temperature. Pour soup into a very large bowl. Add meat to soup pot. Process cold soup in a blender or food processor until uniform in consistency. Pour the blended soup over the meat. Stir and reheat.

Ladle into soups bowls and top with reduced cream, fresh diced scallions and paprika.

Options: Add 1 cup of pre-cooked wild rice when reheating soup.

Serves 8-10

Ruffed Grouse Soup

2 cups cooked, cubed ruffed grouse or smoked turkey breast

1 clove garlic, minced

1/4 cup finely chopped onion

1/4 cup red bell pepper, diced

1 cup sliced carrots

1 cup of broccoli, small florets

1 cup sweet corn kernels

2 Tablespoons butter

1/4 teaspoon freshly ground black pepper

1/4 cup sifted all-purpose white flour

4 cups chicken broth

2 1/2 cups cooked wild rice

2 bay leaves

1 cup cream

1/4 cup red bell peppers, chopped

1/2 cup finely chopped fresh chives

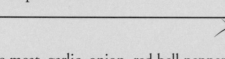

Place meat, garlic, onion, red bell pepper, carrots, broccoli, corn and butter in a large soup pot over medium heat. Sauté until vegetables start to brown. In a bowl combine pepper and flour. Stir one cup of broth into the flour. Blend well. Add this to stockpot along with remaining broth, wild rice and bay leaves. Bring to boil over medium-high heat. Reduce heat and simmer for 30-35 minutes stirring occasionally. Blend in cream and simmer for 10-15 minutes longer. Do not allow soup to boil after adding cream. Remove bay leaves and discard. Ladle into soup bowl.

Garnish with chopped red bell pepper and fresh chives.

Serves 6-8

June 3rd Sunday 1804

"Several Deer Killed to day— at the mouth of the Murow Creek I Saw much Sign of war parties of Inds. haveing Crossed the mouth of this Creek."

William Clark

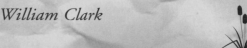

13

Sharpy's Soup

1 large onion, coarsely chopped

1 cup celery, chopped

2 Tablespoons canola oil

2 smoked turkey legs

2 quarts of water

1 small turnip, 1/2-inch dice

2 cups kale, large stems removed, chopped

2 teaspoons chicken bullion

2 Tablespoons ginger, freshly grated

1 teaspoon ground cumin

1 teaspoon ground cardamom

1 teaspoon ground coriander

1 teaspoon dried rosemary

1 bay leaf

2 Tablespoons grapefruit zest

Sauté onions and celery in oil until onions are translucent. Add remaining ingredients. Bring to a rolling boil, reduce heat and simmer one hour, stirring occasionally. Remove turkey legs from soup. Allow to cool. Remove meat from bones, chop into bite size pieces and return to soup. Simmer for 10 minutes and remove from heat. Discard bay leaf.

Serve with your favorite bread and salad.

Serves 6

11th June 1804 Monday

"we had the meat Jurked and also the Venison, which is a Constant Practice to have all the fresh meat not used, Dried in this way."

William Clark

Sgt. Gass' Pepper Jerky Soup

4 cloves garlic, minced

1 large onion, chopped

2 stalks celery, chopped

4 large carrots, sliced

3 Tablespoons of extra virgin olive oil

1 fifteen-ounce can of black beans

1 fifteen-ounce can of kidney beans

1 fifteen-ounce can of pinto beans

1 fifteen-ounce can of navy beans

2 bay leaves

1/4 cup red bell pepper, diced

1 cup of broccoli, small florets

1 teaspoon fresh ground black pepper

7 1/2 cups of chicken stock

2 to 3 ounces of beef jerky, cut into matchsticks

1 cup wild rice, precooked

1 cup scallions, sliced

Saute garlic, onion, celery, and carrots, in olive oil in large soup pot over medium heat. Add the beans with their liquid, bay leaves, red bell pepper, broccoli, pepper and chicken stock. Bring to a boil, then reduce heat to simmer. Cover and simmer for about 1 hour, stirring occasionally. Add jerky and wild rice after 1/2 hour. Remove from heat and discard bay leaves before serving.

Garnish with scallions.

Serves 6-8

Wednesday June 26th 1805

We had some rain last night, and this morning, we had cloudy weather; the party set out early this morning, with their loads to the canoes, it consisted of parched Corn meal, pork, Powder & lead, Axes and Iron tools, Biscuit, Portable soup &ca.

Joseph Whitehouse

Browned Buffalo Bones Soup

2 pounds of soup bones from buffalo (beef bones work well also)
Note: crack bones with hammer to expose as much marrow as possible

1 pound of buffalo round steak, 1-inch cubes (substitute beef)

2 Tablespoons of butter

2 cloves garlic, minced

1 medium onion, chopped

2 stalks celery, sliced

2 medium carrots, sliced

3 Tablespoons butter, (divided in half)

10 cups boiling water

1 cup shredded cabbage

1 fifteen-ounce can of green beans, drained

1 bay leaf

1 teaspoon salt

1 Tablespoon soy sauce

1 teaspoon Worcestershire sauce

3/4 teaspoon dried marjoram

1 quart of tomato juice

cream

Bake bones in an uncovered roasting pan at 375 degrees F for about 25 minutes, until brown. Discard any liquid and set aside bones. In a skillet, brown buffalo in half of the butter. Do not overcook, as buffalo cooks quickly. In a large soup pot, sauté garlic, onion, celery, and carrots in the rest of the butter, until tender. Add browned bones, meat, water, cabbage, beans, bay leaf, salt, soy sauce, Worcestershire sauce, marjoram and tomato juice. Bring to a boil and reduce heat. Cover and simmer 1 1/2 to 2 hours, stirring occasionally. Remove bones from pot. Cool slightly and remove any remaining meat from bones. Discard the bones, returning meat to pot. Simmer uncovered for 45-60 minutes. Remove from heat and discard bay leaf.

Add cream to taste.

Serves 10

Roots Soup

1/4 teaspoon minced garlic

1/2 cup onion, chopped

2 carrots, peeled and chopped

2 Tablespoons butter

4 medium potatoes, peeled and cubed

3 cups water

1/4 teaspoon dried dill weed

1/2 teaspoon salt

1/2 teaspoon fresh ground black pepper

1 cup cream

bacon bits

In a medium sized kettle; sauté garlic, onion, and carrots in butter until onions are translucent. Add potatoes, water, dill, salt and pepper. Simmer until carrots and potato are done (about 20 minutes). Mash the soup mixture with potato masher until soup has a thicker consistency. Soup will not be smooth. Stir in cream and reheat. (Do not let the soup boil after adding the cream). Garnish with crumbled bacon bits and serve.

Serves 4-6

July 19th Thursday 1804
"I call this Island Butter Island, as at this place we mad use of the last of our butter, as we approach this Great River Platt..."

William Clark

Get Well Soup (for a friend)

2 Tablespoons butter

1 small onion, chopped

2 large carrots, large dice

1/2 stalk celery, chopped

2 cups water

1 small potato, peeled and diced

1/8 teaspoon dried ginger

1/4 teaspoon ground thyme

1/8 teaspoon ground nutmeg

1/4 teaspoon salt

1/2 teaspoon fresh ground black pepper

1/2 teaspoon dried dill weed

2 cups chopped asparagus, 1/2-inch pieces

2 teaspoons chicken bouillon

1/2 cup cream

Sauté onion, carrots and celery in butter until onions are translucent. Add water, potatoes, ginger, thyme, nutmeg, salt, pepper and dill weed. Simmer for 20 minutes or until potatoes are tender. Add asparagus and simmer for 10 more minutes. Add chicken bouillon and cream. Simmer an additional 5 minutes. Do not allow soup to boil after adding cream.

Garnish with croutons.

Serves 4-6

Monday June 17th 1805

"The Indian woman much better today, I have still continued the same course of medecine; she is free from pain clear of fever, her pulse regular, and eats heartily as I am willing to permit her of broiled buffaloe well seasoned with pepper and salt and rich soope of the same meat; I think therefore that there is every rational hope of her recovery."

Meriwether Lewis

157. *The Missouri below the Mouth of the Platte*, watercolor on paper, 8 3/4 X 10 3/4

151. *Nodaway Island*, watercolor on paper, 8 ¾ X 10 ¾

Crab and Mushroom Muffins

3/4 cup of butter

1 eight-ounce package chive-flavored cream cheese

1/4 teaspoon minced garlic

1 teaspoon finely chopped parsley

1 six-ounce can of crab meat, drained

8-10 fresh mushrooms, chopped

12 English muffins, split in half and lightly toasted

Seafood seasoning

In a medium saucepan over medium low heat add butter, cream cheese and garlic. Stir until melted and blended. Add parsley, crab and mushrooms, stirring until mushrooms are coated. Spread mixture evenly on muffins. Place on a cookie sheet and broil until slightly browned. Lightly sprinkle with seafood seasoning.

Yield: 24 muffin halves

[Weather, June 1805] in the remarks

15th   The deer now begin to bring forth their young   the young Magpies begin to fly.

Lewis and Clark

Crab Dip

1/4 cup salad dressing

1/8 teaspoon ground cayenne pepper

3 Tablespoons milk

1 clove garlic, finely minced

1 eight-ounce package of cream cheese with chives, softened

1 six-ounce can of crab meat, drained

fresh parsley leaves

ground paprika

In a bowl combine the salad dressing, cayenne, milk, garlic and cream cheese. Combine crabmeat with cheese mixture. Sprinkle with parsley and paprika.

Serve with chips or fresh veggies.

Yield: about 2 cups

Elk Tortilla Pinwheels

1 pound ground elk (substitute buffalo or lean beef)

1 Tablespoon prepared mustard

1 envelope dry onion soup mix

1/4-teaspoon fresh ground black pepper

1 clove garlic, minced

1 cup shredded Cheddar cheese

1/2 cup shredded Mozzarella cheese

3-4 nine-inch flour tortillas

1 cup sour cream

1 cup salsa

Using a cast iron skillet, brown the meat with the mustard, onion soup mix, pepper, and garlic. Stir thoroughly. Drain fat. Add Cheddar and Mozzarella cheeses to meat mixture. Remove from heat. Spread sour cream evenly on tortillas. Spread meat mixture over entire tortilla, one at a time. Add dabs of salsa across tortilla. Roll tortilla up, securing with a half dozen toothpicks evenly spaced. Slice between toothpicks to make pinwheels. Secure each pinwheel with an additional toothpick at a ninety-degree angle. Arrange on plate and microwave to warm before serving.

Yield: about 30 pinwheels

Spicy Buffalo Triangles

1/2 pound ground buffalo (substitute elk or lean beef)

1/2 cup chopped onion

1/2 teaspoon salt

1/2 teaspoon fresh ground black pepper

2 finely minced cloves of garlic

1/2 teaspoon ground thyme

1 six-ounce can tomato paste

12 stuffed green olives, coarsely chopped

1 jalapeno pepper, seeded and chopped

1/4 teaspoon ground cayenne pepper (optional)

1/2 cup well-drained sauerkraut

1 cup Colby cheese, grated

1 stick butter (1/4 pound)

1/2 pound phyllo dough

Brown the meat in a large skillet; stir in the onion, salt and black pepper (buffalo cooks quicker than beef). The onion should be tender but not soft. Add garlic, thyme, tomato paste, olives, jalapeno pepper, cayenne and sauerkraut. Simmer, covered for 30 minutes, adding small amounts of water if necessary. Remove from heat and allow mixture to cool. Add Colby cheese. Melt butter over low heat in small saucepan. Remove butter from heat. Unroll phyllo dough and cut into 1-1/2 inch strips. Phyllo dough dries very quickly and then cracks easily, so dampen a towel and keep dough covered when not in use. Take out one piece at a time and brush it with melted butter. Place one spoonful of mixture at end of dough strip and fold corner over forming a triangle. Now keep folding, like a flag, until you reach the end of the dough. You should have a neat triangle at the end. Use a butter-flavored cooking spray to coat the cookie sheet. Apply melted butter to the tops of the triangles. Cover cookie sheet with plastic wrap and place in refrigerator for 1 hour. Bake in preheated oven (400 degrees F) for about 20 minutes, or until golden brown.

Yield: about 14 triangles

Smoked Salmon Canapés

1 eight-ounce package cream cheese

zest of 1 lime

1 teaspoon dried, minced onion

1 teaspoon Worcestershire sauce

1 fresh scallion, minced

1 Tablespoon fresh ground black
    pepper (more if needed)

1/2 teaspoon dried crushed basil leaves

1/4 teaspoon ground cayenne pepper

1 pound jicama, peeled

3 lime wedges

1/2 pound smoked salmon

Combine cheese, lime zest, onion, Worcestershire sauce and scallion in a small mixing bowl. Beat at medium speed with an electric mixer until smooth. Set aside. Mix black pepper, basil and cayenne pepper together on a small saucer and set aside. Cut jicama into 1/4-inch thick slices and peel. Cut slices into 2-inch squares. Cut each square in half diagonally to make triangles. Rub the longest side of each triangle with a lime wedge. Dip this side of each triangle in black pepper, basil and cayenne pepper mixture. Repeat procedure with remaining triangles. Spoon a little of the cheese mixture onto each triangle. Top with a small piece of salmon.

Yield: at least 24 triangles

Thursday March 13 1806

"the common Salmon and red Charr are the inhabitants of both the sea and rivers. the former is usually largest and weighs from 5 to 15 lbs. it is this speceis that extends itself into all the rivers and little creeks on this side of the Continent, and to which the natives are so much indebted for their subsistence."

Meriwether Lewis

27

Easy Cheesy Salsa Dip

1/2 pound lean ground venison (substitute beef or buffalo)

1 teaspoon roasted garlic, minced

1/4 teaspoon ground cumin

1 sixteen-ounce jar of salsa

1 jalapeno pepper, seeded and chopped

1 six-ounce can of tomato sauce

1 four-and-one half-ounce can of chopped green chilies, drained

1/4 cup sliced black olives

1/2 pound processed cheese loaf cut into 1-inch cubes

1/4 cup sliced scallions (whites and greens)

Place the venison in a microwave-proof bowl. Set microwave on high for 4 minutes. Stir and microwave again until meat is done. Do not over cook. Meat should be an even and loose consistency. Place meat in colander and rinse with hot water to remove excess fat. Return meat to microwave bowl. Add garlic, cumin, salsa, pepper, tomato sauce, chilies, olives, and cheese. Mix well. Microwave on high until cheese is melted and mixture is hot (approximately 5 minutes). Stir thoroughly.

Garnish with scallions. Serve with chips.

Yield: about 3 cups

Monday July 29th 1805

"This morning some of the hunters turned out and returned in a few hours with four fat bucks, the venison is now very fine."

Meriwether Lewis

Blackfoot Pâté

2 eight-ounce packages cream cheese, softened

1/8 teaspoon ground cayenne pepper

1/2 teaspoon coarsely ground black pepper

1/2 teaspoon seasoned salt

1 teaspoon roasted garlic, minced

1 teaspoon hot pepper sauce

1 teaspoon extra virgin olive oil

2 teaspoons chopped fresh cilantro

2 Tablespoons Worcestershire sauce

1/3 cup thick and chunky salsa

1/2 cup scallions, chopped

2 1/4-ounce packages of gelatin, unflavored

2 fifteen-ounce cans black beans, drained

several dark lettuce leaves

1 eight-ounce container sour cream

1 four-ounce jar pimientos, well drained and diced

1 Tablespoon minced fresh parsley

Combine cream cheese, cayenne pepper, black pepper, salt, garlic, pepper sauce, gelatin, olive oil, cilantro, Worcestershire sauce, salsa, scallions and beans in a food processor or blender. Blend for one minute, or until mixture is creamy. Spoon into large bowl lined with lettuce leaves. Refrigerate for three hours. Top with sour cream, pimientos and parsley.

Serve with thick corn chips or tortilla chips.

Yield: about 4 1/2 cups

Stuffed Portabellas with Sun-dried Tomatoes

3 medium to large fresh portabella mushrooms

1/4 cup extra virgin olive oil

1/3 cup salsa

1 ten-ounce package of spinach, thawed and squeezed dry

1/4 cup grated Parmesan cheese

1/3 cup sun-dried tomatoes packed in oil, drained and chopped

1/2 cup minced scallions

1/4 teaspoon ground cayenne pepper

1 cup of shredded Mozzarella cheese

Preheat oven to 375 degrees F. Clean mushrooms and remove stems. Allow to dry. Coat tops of mushrooms with oil. Place gill side down in baking pan. Bake for ten minutes. Combine salsa, spinach, Parmesan cheese, sun dried tomatoes, scallions and cayenne pepper in a bowl. Place mushrooms gill side up in baking pan. Spoon mixture onto mushrooms. Sprinkle with shredded mozzarella cheese. Heat in oven until cheese is melted. Cut into quarters and serve immediately.

Serves 3-4

Stuffed Mushrooms with Roasted Pine Nuts

2 Tablespoons extra virgin olive oil

1/2 teaspoon hot pepper sauce

1 one-and-three-quarter-ounce jar of pine nuts

seasoned salt

24 medium to large fresh white mushrooms

1 Tablespoon extra virgin olive oil

1 1/2 teaspoons minced roasted garlic

4 Tablespoons scallions, diced fine

1 small portabella mushroom, finely chopped

1/4 cup sun-dried tomatoes packed in oil, hand squeezed, drained, chopped

1/2 teaspoon dried basil leaves

1/8 teaspoon fresh ground black pepper

1 cup Feta cheese, crumbled

In a large skillet combine 1 Tablespoon oil and hot pepper sauce over low heat. Add pine nuts. Gradually increase heat until oil is very hot. Stir constantly. When pine nuts begin to turn brown remove from oil and drain. Sprinkle with seasoned salt. Lay out on paper towels and pat dry. Preheat oven to 375 degrees F. Remove stems and clean both white mushrooms and the portabellas. Allow white mushrooms to dry and dice portabellas. Set portabellas aside. Coat a broiling pan with butter-flavored cooking spray. Place white mushrooms on broiler pan with tops facing up. Spray mushrooms with butter-flavored spray. Bake for 15 minutes or until tender and set aside. In a small skillet add 1 tablespoon oil, garlic, scallions and finely chopped portabella mushroom. Sauté until tender. No liquid should be present. Combine with pine nuts, sun-dried tomatoes, basil and pepper. In a medium bowl combine mixture with Feta cheese. Taking two spoons, stuff mushrooms with cheese mixture. Bake for 15 minutes. Serve hot.

Yield: 24 mushrooms

Deviled Eggs

8 hard boiled eggs

3 Tablespoons salad dressing

1 teaspoon mustard

1 teaspoon granulated white sugar

Dash of salt

1/4 teaspoon ground paprika

Boil eggs for twenty minutes. Allow to cool in cold water. Peel eggs and cut in half lengthwise. Place yolks in small bowl. Place whites open face on platter. Mash yolks with fork until crumbly. Stir in remaining ingredients and blend until smooth. Place spoonfuls of yolk mixture in each egg white half. Sprinkle tops with paprika. Chill and serve.

Yield: 16 pieces

Spicy Crab Chip Dip

4 ounces cream cheese

1 Tablespoon butter

1 clove garlic, minced

1 Tablespoon grated Parmesan cheese

1/4 teaspoon seafood seasoning

1/4 teaspoon dry mustard

1 six-ounce can crab meat

1 Tablespoon salad dressing

1 cup shredded Cheddar cheese

fresh parsley leaves, minced

Microwave cream cheese and butter on low until soft. Stir in garlic, Parmesan cheese, seafood seasoning, mustard, crab meat and salad dressing. Place in ovenproof dish. Sprinkle Cheddar on mixture and broil in oven until cheese is melted.

Garnish with parsley

Serve with chips or fresh vegetables.

Yield: about 2 cups

Artichoke Dip

1 cup salad dressing

1 fourteen-ounce can artichoke hearts, chopped, drained

1 cup grated Parmesan cheese

1/2 teaspoon fresh basil, chopped

1 Tablespoon sun-dried tomatoes in oil, small dice

1 clove garlic, minced

Combine all ingredients and refrigerate for at least one hour.

Serve with crackers and chips.

Yield: 2 1/2 cups

Tuesday April 9 1805

"when we halted for dinner the squaw busied herself in serching for the wild artichokes which the mice collect and deposit in large hoards.   this operation she performed by penetrating the earth with a sharp stick about some small collections of drift wood. her labour soon proved successful, and she procurrd a good quantity of these roots."

Meriwether Lewis

"Buffalo Chip" Dip

1 pound ground buffalo (substitute elk or lean ground beef)

1/2 cup chili sauce

1 package taco seasoning

1/4 teaspoon ground cayenne pepper

1 sixteen-ounce can of refried beans with chilies

1/2 cup sour cream with chives

1 six-ounce can of black olives, sliced

1/4 cup onions, chopped

1 cup Cheddar cheese, shredded

1 scallion, sliced

Brown buffalo in a heavy skillet over a low heat. Don't overcook. Add chili sauce and taco seasoning (follow package instructions). Let cool when done. Mix cayenne with beans, stirring thoroughly. On a plate, make a layer of each of the following: bean mixture, buffalo mixture, sour cream, olives, onions, cheese and scallions.

Serve with corn chips.

Serves 4-6

June 3, 1805

"Capt. C & myself stroled out to the top of the hights in the fork of these rivers from whence we had an extensive and most inchanting view; the country in every derection around us was one vast plain in which innumberable herds of Buffalow were seen attended by their sheppards the wolves;"

Meriwether Lewis

Clatsop Crab Dip

2 eight-ounce packages cream cheese, softened

1 teaspoon horseradish

2 Tablespoons salad dressing

1 teaspoon seafood seasoning

1/2 pound imitation crab meat pieces

1/4 cup cocktail sauce

1/2 cup scallions

3/4 cup fresh tomatoes, diced and seeded

1 six-ounce can black olives, sliced, drained

1/2 cup Cheddar cheese, shredded

Combine cream cheese with horseradish, salad dressing, and seafood seasoning. Mix thoroughly. On a plate make a layer of each as follows: cream cheese, crab, cocktail sauce, scallions, tomatoes, olives, and cheese.

Serve with your favorite chips.

Serves 4-6

185. *Sioux Camp*, watercolor on paper, 7 1/2 X 10 3/8

309. *Máhchsi-Karéhde, Mandan Man,* watercolor and pencil on paper, 16 7/8 X 12

Breads, Biscuits & Dumplings

Sunday 22nd Sept. 1805

"the natives gave us Such food as they had to eat, consisting of roots of different kinds which was Sweet and good also red & black haws & c. the principal roots which they made use off for food are pleanty. this praries are covred with them they are much like potatoes when cooked, and they have a curious way of cooking them. th[e]y have places made in form of a Small coal pit, & they heat Stone in the pit. then put Straw over the Stone, then water to raise a Steem. then they put on large loves of the pounded potatoes, and 8 or 10 bushels of potatoes on at once then cover them with wet Straw and Earth. in that way they Sweet them untill they are cooked, and when they take them out they pound Some of them up fine and make them in loaves and cakes. they dry the cakes and String them on Strings, in Such a way that they would keep a year & handy to carry, any journey."

Joseph Whitehouse

St. Louis Buttermilk Corn Bread

1 cup sifted all-purpose white flour

1/8 teaspoon ground nutmeg

1/2 teaspoon salt

1/4 cup granulated white sugar

4 teaspoons baking powder

1 cup yellow cornmeal (preferably stone ground)

2 eggs, beaten

1/4 teaspoon butter flavoring

1/2 cup buttermilk

1/2 cup milk

1/4 cup corn oil

Preheat oven to 375 degrees F. Sift flour, nutmeg, salt, sugar, baking powder and cornmeal together in a medium bowl. In a separate bowl, combine the eggs, butter flavoring, buttermilk, milk and oil. Add dry ingredients to wet and beat quickly until batter is smooth. Pour batter into an oiled 9x9-inch baking pan. Bake for 20-25 minutes, or until a knife inserted in the center comes out clean. Remove from oven and cool pan on rack for at least 10 minutes. Using a regular table knife, cut the cornbread into squares.

Serve hot as a side to a main dish or with butter, syrup and a sprinkle of cinnamon.

Yield: 9 large squares

Harvest Squash Bread

1/2 cup corn oil

3/4 cup granulated white sugar

1 1/2 teaspoons vanilla extract

2 eggs, beaten

1/4 teaspoon salt

1 1/2 teaspoons baking powder

1/2 teaspoon baking soda

2-3 teaspoons pumpkin pie spice

1 1/2 cups sifted all-purpose white flour

1/2 cup pecans, chopped

1 1/2 cups peeled, cooked butternut squash

Preheat the oven to 350 degrees F. Combine oil, sugar, vanilla and eggs in a bowl. Blend until mixture is smooth. In a separate bowl sift salt, baking powder, soda, pumpkin pie spice and flour. Add flour mixture to wet mixture and combine only until all dry ingredients are incorporated. Add pecans and squash. Mix thoroughly. Pour into an oiled 9x5-inch loaf pan and bake 40-50 minutes, until a knife inserted comes out clean. Remove from heat and cool on rack to room temperature (about 40 minutes).

Serve with cream cheese and fresh sliced strawberries.

Yield: 1 loaf

Sourdough Starter

1 package active dry yeast
2 3/4 cups lukewarm water
3 1/4 cups sifted all-purpose white flour

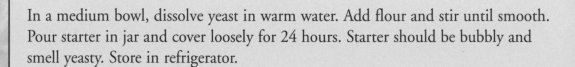

In a medium bowl, dissolve yeast in warm water. Add flour and stir until smooth. Pour starter in jar and cover loosely for 24 hours. Starter should be bubbly and smell yeasty. Store in refrigerator.

Each week remove a cup of starter, even if you aren't going to bake. This will keep the starter fresh. For every cup of starter used, add 1 cup flour and 3/4 cup water to the jar. Always leave at least 1 cup of starter in the jar to keep starter active.

August 3rd. Friday 1804-
"The air is pure and helthy So far as we can Judge."

William Clark

42

Sourdough Bread

Day 1
1 cup sourdough starter

1/2 teaspoon butter flavoring

2 cups lukewarm water

2 cups sifted all-purpose white flour

Combine starter, flavoring, water and flour in large bowl. Cover loosely and let stand in a warm place overnight.

Day 2
1 teaspoon salt

1/2 teaspoon baking powder

2 Tablespoons granulated white sugar

3 Tablespoons canola oil

5-6 cups sifted all-purpose white flour

Butter

Sift salt and baking powder, into sourdough mixture. Add sugar, oil, and 2 cups of sifted flour. Mix well. Add remaining flour as needed. Knead until smooth. Butter top of dough and bottom of bowl. Let stand in a warm place, covered, for 2 hours. Punch down and divide into 2 parts, forming 2 round loaves. Place loaves on oiled baking sheets and set in warm place for 1 hour. Bake at 350 degrees F for 1 hour, until golden brown. Remove from oven and brush tops with butter.

Serve slices warm with butter.

Yield: 2 loaves

Lakota Fry Bread

2 1/2 cups sifted all-purpose white flour

5 teaspoons baking powder

1 1/2 Tablespoons granulated white sugar

1/2 teaspoon salt

1/4 teaspoon ground mace

1/4 teaspoon ground allspice

1 Tablespoon canola oil

1 egg, beaten

1/4 teaspoon vanilla extract

3/4 cup water

canola oil for frying

Sift dry ingredients in a mixing bowl. In separate bowl combine oil, egg, vanilla and water. Stir in flour mixture and then knead bread until the dough is smooth. Let dough rest for 5 minutes. Roll out to 1/2-inch thickness and cut pieces into desired shape and size. Fry in hot oil.

Serve hot with your favorite soup or stew, or with butter and honey.

Yield: varies with size of pieces

November 30 Saturday 1805

"The Squar, gave me a piece of Bread to day made of Some flower She had Cearfully kept for her child, and had unfortunately got wet—"

William Clark

Grandma's Sourdough Biscuits

1 cup sifted all-purpose white flour

1/4 teaspoon garlic powder

1/2 teaspoon baking soda

1/2 teaspoon salt

1/2 teaspoon dried dill weed

2 teaspoons baking powder

1 cup sourdough starter

1/4 cup buttermilk

1/2 teaspoon butter flavoring

3 Tablespoons corn oil or melted butter

Preheat the oven to 350 degrees F. Combine flour, garlic powder, baking soda, salt, dill and baking powder in a bowl. Make a well in the center and add the starter, buttermilk, butter flavoring and oil or butter. Mix until a stiff dough is formed. Turn the dough out onto a floured board and knead briefly until the dough is smooth. This dough is supposed to be a little sticky, so do not over knead. Spoon biscuits onto a greased cookie sheet. Let stand in warm place for 40 minutes. Bake for 30 minutes. Brush with melted butter.

For regular biscuits, omit garlic and dill.

Yield: 12-15 biscuits

Spiced Wild Rice Bread

1 1/3 cups sifted all-purpose white
    flour

1/2 teaspoon baking soda

1 teaspoon salt

1/4 cup corn meal

2 Tablespoons pine nuts, crushed

2 Tablespoons butter, softened

1/4 cup maple syrup

2 eggs, beaten

1 1/2 cups buttermilk

1/2 cup milk

1 cup cooked wild rice

Preheat the oven to 325 degrees F. Sift flour, soda, salt and corn meal together in a medium mixing bowl. Add pine nuts. In a large bowl blend butter and maple syrup. Mix in eggs and stir until creamy. Add buttermilk, milk and wild rice to butter mixture. Add dry ingredients to butter mixture and mix until combined. Pour the dough into a greased 9x9-inch baking pan and bake for 60 minutes. Remove from heat and allow the bread to cool to room temperature (about 40 minutes).

Serve with cream cheese and fresh fruit.

Yield: 9-12 pieces

Wednesday 20th September 1805
"...they [those people] gave us a Small piece of Buffalow meat, Some dried Salmon beries & roots in different States, Some round and much like an onion which they call [Pas she co] quamash the Bread or Cake is called Pas-she-co Sweet, of this they make bread & Supe they also gave us the bread made of this root all of which we eate hartily,"

William Clark

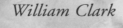

Wedding Waffles

1 cup sifted all-purpose white flour

1 cup stirred whole wheat flour

1 teaspoon baking soda

1 Tablespoon wheat germ

1/2 teaspoon salt

1 3/4 cups milk

2 Tablespoons apple cider vinegar

2 eggs, beaten

1/4 cup canola oil

1 teaspoon vanilla extract

2 teaspoons honey

Mix white flour, wheat flour, soda, wheat germ and salt in a bowl. Stir in milk, vinegar, eggs, oil, vanilla and then the honey. Mix until moistened. Mixture will be a little lumpy. Spoon batter onto a hot waffle iron. Close and bake until steaming stops (about 4 minutes)

Yield: 5 or 6 waffles

Corn Dodgers

5 strips bacon

2 1/2 Tablespoons bacon drippings or
    corn oil

1 cup sifted all-purpose white flour

1 cup cornmeal

1 teaspoon baking powder

1/2 teaspoon baking soda

1/2 teaspoon salt

1 teaspoon apple cider vinegar

1 teaspoon vanilla extract

1/4 cup maple syrup

1 egg, beaten

1 cup buttermilk (as needed)

Preheat oven to 375 degrees F. Fry bacon in cast iron frying pan until crisp. Remove bacon and reserve. Pour off bacon fat. Rinse frying pan with warm water briefly. Melt butter in frying pan. Sift dry ingredients into a bowl. Add melted butter and remaining ingredients to dry mixture. Stir until moistened. Pour batter into frying pan and bake for 1/2 hour, or until a toothpick inserted comes out clean.

Cut into wedges and serve with butter, syrup and crumbled bacon.

Yield: 6-8 wedges

11th October Thursday 1804-
"Those people gave us to eate bread made of Corn & Beens, also Corn & Beans boild. a large Been (of) which they rob the mice of the Prarie (who collect & discover it) which is rich & verry nurrishing also [S] quashes & c. all Tranquillity."

William Clark

Almond and Pear Bread

2 cups sifted all-purpose white flour

2 1/2 teaspoons baking powder

1/4 teaspoon salt

1/2 teaspoon ground cinnamon

1/4 teaspoon ground nutmeg

1/2 cup butter

1/2 cup dark brown sugar

1/2 cup granulated white sugar

2 eggs, beaten

1 teaspoon vanilla extract

1/4 cup sour cream

1/2 teaspoon lemon zest

2/3 cup slivered almonds

1 1/2 cups ripe pears, cored, peeled and chopped

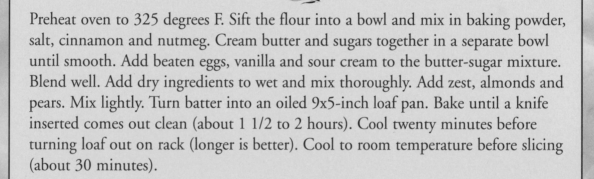

Preheat oven to 325 degrees F. Sift the flour into a bowl and mix in baking powder, salt, cinnamon and nutmeg. Cream butter and sugars together in a separate bowl until smooth. Add beaten eggs, vanilla and sour cream to the butter-sugar mixture. Blend well. Add dry ingredients to wet and mix thoroughly. Add zest, almonds and pears. Mix lightly. Turn batter into an oiled 9x5-inch loaf pan. Bake until a knife inserted comes out clean (about 1 1/2 to 2 hours). Cool twenty minutes before turning loaf out on rack (longer is better). Cool to room temperature before slicing (about 30 minutes).

Serve with a scoop of vanilla ice cream on each slice.

Yield: 1 loaf

Corn Meal Buns

1 package dry yeast
1/4 cup warm water
1/2 teaspoon granulated white sugar

Combine yeast, water and sugar in a medium bowl. Set in warm place until ready to use.

---

2 cups milk
1/4 cup butter

In medium sauce pan scald the milk over medium heat. Remove from heat and add butter. Set aside and allow to cool.

1/4 cup canola oil
1/2 cup granulated white sugar
1 teaspoon salt
1/4 teaspoon vanilla extract
1/2 teaspoon maple flavoring
1/4 teaspoon ground nutmeg
 2 eggs, beaten

In a large bowl combine the oil, sugar, salt and flavorings. Stir in the milk mixture, beaten eggs, and yeast mixture.

---

1 1/2 cups corn meal
7 1/2 cups sifted all-purpose white
    flour (approximately)

Add corn meal and 3 cups of flour to liquid. Stir. Keep on adding flour, hand kneading when the dough is too thick to stir. Knead until dough is smooth and satin like. Grease bowl and top of dough. Let rise in warm place until dough doubles in size, about 1 to 1 1/2 hours. Punch down and shape into buns and place on greased baking sheet. Let rise until doubled, about another hour. Bake in preheated oven at 375 degrees F. for 15 minutes. Brush rolls with butter.

Yield: about 30 buns

Basic Biscuits

5 cups sifted all purpose white flour

6 teaspoons baking powder

1 Tablespoon granulated white sugar

1 teaspoon salt

2 sticks (1/2 pound) butter, softened

1 1/4 cups cold milk (as needed)

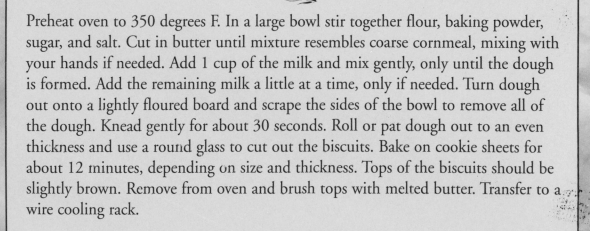

Preheat oven to 350 degrees F. In a large bowl stir together flour, baking powder, sugar, and salt. Cut in butter until mixture resembles coarse cornmeal, mixing with your hands if needed. Add 1 cup of the milk and mix gently, only until the dough is formed. Add the remaining milk a little at a time, only if needed. Turn dough out onto a lightly floured board and scrape the sides of the bowl to remove all of the dough. Knead gently for about 30 seconds. Roll or pat dough out to an even thickness and use a round glass to cut out the biscuits. Bake on cookie sheets for about 12 minutes, depending on size and thickness. Tops of the biscuits should be slightly brown. Remove from oven and brush tops with melted butter. Transfer to a wire cooling rack.

Serve warm.

Yield: 20-30 biscuits, depending on size

Rye Crackers

1 cup sifted all-purpose white flour
1/2 cup stirred stone ground dark rye flour
1 1/2 teaspoons baking powder
1/2 teaspoon salt
4 Tablespoons cold butter, diced
1/2 cup ice water (as needed)

In a bowl, mix together the flours, baking powder and salt. Cut in the butter until the mixture resembles coarse cornmeal. Add the ice water a little at a time until the dough is just formed. Do not over mix. Cover the top of the bowl with plastic food wrap and place in the refrigerator for 30 minutes. Remove dough from the refrigerator and, on a floured surface, shape the dough as desired. For round crackers, shape into a log. For rectangles, you can place plastic food wrap inside a small loaf pan and simply press the dough in gently. Cover your shaped dough in plastic food wrap and place in the freezing compartment for at least 30 minutes. The dough should be quite firm but not completely frozen. Preheat oven to 350 degrees F. Unwrap dough and cut quickly into 1/8-inch thick slices and place them on a baking sheet. If you desire salted tops, brush each cracker with water and sprinkle with a little bit of salt. Bake for about 15 minutes, until crackers have browned slightly and are crisp. Remove from heat and transfer the crackers to a cooling rack.

Serve with your favorite soup or stew.

Yield: 20-24 2-inch crackers

Berry Spoon Biscuits

2 cups sifted all-purpose white flour

3 Tablespoons granulated white sugar

2 teaspoons baking powder

1/4 cup butter

1 egg, beaten

3/4 cup milk

1 teaspoon vanilla extract

1/2 teaspoon butter flavoring

1/2 cup dried berries

2 Tablespoons granulated white sugar

1/4 cup pecans, chopped

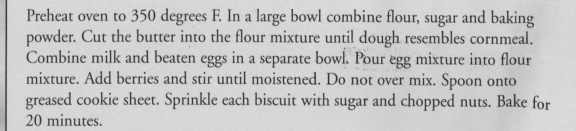

Preheat oven to 350 degrees F. In a large bowl combine flour, sugar and baking powder. Cut the butter into the flour mixture until dough resembles cornmeal. Combine milk and beaten eggs in a separate bowl. Pour egg mixture into flour mixture. Add berries and stir until moistened. Do not over mix. Spoon onto greased cookie sheet. Sprinkle each biscuit with sugar and chopped nuts. Bake for 20 minutes.

Yield: about 2 dozen

Tuesday 10 December 1805

"...I purchased a little of the berry bread and a fiew of their roots for which I gave Small fish hooks, which they appeared fond of—..."

William Clark

Cheese Biscuits

1/2 pound medium Cheddar cheese, grated (about 2 cups)

2 cloves garlic, minced

1 teaspoon parsley, chopped

1/4 cup green olives, pitted, sliced and drained

1 cup butter, softened

2 cups sifted all-purpose white flour

2 teaspoons baking powder

1/2 teaspoon ground cayenne pepper

1/2 teaspoon seafood seasoning

3/4 cup cold milk (as needed)

Preheat oven to 350 degrees F. Mix grated cheese, garlic, parsley, olives and butter in a bowl. Add flour, baking powder, pepper and seafood seasoning. Mix well. Add only enough milk to form dough. Allow the dough (covered) to rest in the refrigerator for 30 minutes. Drop spoonfuls of biscuit batter onto cookie sheet. Bake for 30 minutes.

Yield: about 2 dozen

Monday January 26th 1806

"the natives either eat these berrys when ripe immediately from the bushes or dryed in the sun or by means of their sw{e}ating kilns; very frequently they pound them and bake then in large loaves of 10 or fifteen pounds; this bread keeps very well during one season and retains the moist jeucies of the fruit much better than by any other method of preservation. this bread is broken and stired in could water until it be sufficiently thick and then eaten; in this way the natives most generally use it."

Meriwether Lewis

182. *Bijoux Hills on the Missouri*, watercolor and pencil on paper, 9 5/8 X 12 1/4

257. *Kiäsax, Piegan Blackfeet Man,* watercolor on paper, 12 1/4 X 9 1/2

Beans, Salads & Vegetables

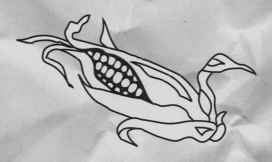

Monday July 22cd 1805

"I passed though a large Island which I found a beautifull level and fertile plain about 10 feet above the surface of the water and never overflown.   on this Island I met with great quantities of a smal onion about the size of a musquit ball and some even larger; they were white crisp and well flavored   I geathered about half a bushel of them before the canoes arrived."

Meriwether Lewis

Arikara Autumn Chowder

1 small leek, chopped

1 Tablespoon butter

2 medium potatoes, cubed

1 medium carrot, sliced

2 cups water

1/2 teaspoon salt

1 cup cooked pumpkin (squash may be substituted)

1 teaspoon dried basil leaves

1/2 teaspoon dried mustard

1 Tablespoon apple cider vinegar

1 fifteen-ounce can cream style corn

1 cup heavy cream

In large dutch oven, sauté leeks in butter until translucent. Add potatoes, carrots, water and salt. When potatoes are tender add pumpkin and mash carefully or puree if desired. Add basil, mustard, vinegar, corn and cream. Reheat if necessary.

Garnish with roasted and salted sunflower nuts.

Serves 6

Creole Kale

1/4 cup green onions, chopped

1/4 cup celery, chopped

1/4 cup red bell pepper, diced

1 Tablespoon butter

1 1/2 teaspoons Cajun seasoning

2 1/4 cups low salt chicken broth

1 cup white rice

2 cups kale with large stems and ribs removed, firmly packed

1 cup peanuts, shelled, roasted and salted

1 cup salad shrimp, cooked

In a large saucepan, sauté onions, celery and pepper in butter until tender. Add Cajun seasoning and broth and bring to a rolling boil. Add rice and kale. Reduce heat and simmer until rice is tender and liquid is absorbed. Set aside for five minutes to let the flavors mingle, then add in peanuts and shrimp.

Serve immediately.

Serves 4

[undated, winter 1804-5] part 3: Botanical Collections
"No. 6 Was taken on the 27th of may 1804 near the mouth of the Gasconade; it is a species of rape or kail, it grows, on the beach of the river, when young my men used it a boiled green and found healthy and pleasent.—"

Meriwether Lewis

Grandma's Picnic Potato Salad

5 medium red potatoes, boiled, peeled and cubed

1/2 cup extra virgin olive oil

2 Tablespoons apple cider vinegar

1 Tablespoon water

1 teaspoon white granulated sugar

1/2 teaspoon salt

4 scallions, finely chopped

fresh ground black pepper to taste

several dark green lettuce leaves

2 Tablespoons bacon, crisp fried and finely crumbled

Place cubed potatoes in a large mixing bowl. In a separate bowl, whisk together the oil, vinegar, water, sugar and salt. Add the liquid to the potatoes followed by the scallions. Toss lightly, add the pepper and toss lightly again. Line a serving bowl with the dark green lettuce leaves and spoon the potato salad into the lettuce-lined bowl. Spread the crumbled bacon over the top and serve immediately.

Serves 4-6

Métis Bean Salad

1 cup of water

1/2 teaspoon lemon juice

1/2 cup white rice

3 teaspoons ground thyme

1 cup canned kidney beans, drained

1/4 cup celery, chopped

1 cup tomatoes, seeded and diced

1/4 cup sweet corn kernels

1 cup yellow bell pepper, seeded and chopped

1 scallion, minced

1/4 cup bottled Italian dressing

1/2 teaspoon ground cayenne pepper

Bring water to a rolling boil. Add lemon, rice and one teaspoon of thyme. Cover and reduce heat to low. Cook for about 20 minutes until rice is done. Set aside and allow to cool. Turn rice into a mixing bowl, fluffing with a fork. Add beans, celery, tomatoes, corn and pepper to rice. In a small bowl add scallions, dressing, cayenne and the remaining 2 teaspoons of thyme. Whisk until blended thoroughly. Add to salad and toss liberally.

Serves 4

A Peppered Bean Salad

2 teaspoons apple cider vinegar

1/4 cup extra virgin olive oil

1 teaspoon ground oregano

2 teaspoons granulated white sugar

2 sixteen-ounce cans kidney beans, drained

1/2 cup red bell pepper, diced

1/2 cup green bell pepper, diced

1/4 cup red onion, chopped

1/4 cup scallions, sliced thin

In a bowl whisk vinegar and oil together until blended. Add in oregano and sugar. Combine with remaining ingredients. Mix until well coated. Cover and refrigerate overnight.

Garnish with Parmesan cheese.

Serves 6-8 as a side salad

Spicy Potato Salad

3-4 red potatoes, boiled, peeled, quarter-sliced

1/2 cup red onions, diced

4 scallions, sliced thin

1/4 cup rice vinegar, divided

1 pound spicy sausage links, sliced

1/2 cup canola oil

2 teaspoons roasted garlic, minced

1/2 teaspoon ground cayenne pepper

1/2 teaspoon salt

black pepper to taste

Combine potatoes, onions, scallions and 3 tablespoons of vinegar in a large serving bowl. Over medium-low heat brown the sausage in a frying pan with the oil. Remove from pan and allow to cool. Add to potatoes. In same frying pan, add remaining ingredients and remaining tablespoon of vinegar. Reheat while stirring constantly. Pour over salad and toss.

Serves 4-6

Friday April the 12th 1805

"found a great quantity of small onions in the plain where we encamped; had some of them collected and cooked, found them agreeable."

Meriwether Lewis

Marinated Roots and Vegetables

<u>Marinade</u>
1/2 cup extra virgin olive oil

1/3 cup Tamari (soy sauce)

1/4 cup lime juice

2 Tablespoons Dijon mustard

2 Tablespoons Worcestershire sauce

1 teaspoon roasted garlic, minced

1/4 teaspoon ground cayenne pepper

In a bowl, whisk together all marinade ingredients. Set aside.

2 cups potatoes, peeled, 1-inch dice

2 cups of carrots, 1-inch thick slices

1 cup onions, chopped

1 cup broccoli florets

1 cup cauliflower florets

In a cooking bag, mix vegetables and marinade together. Place bag on a roasting pan. Marinate in refrigerator for 30 minutes. Occasionally roll the bag over to coat vegetables. Bake in preheated oven at 325 degrees F for 90 minutes. Take vegetables out of cooking bag and place in serving dish.

Garnish with chives and parsley.

Serve as a side dish.

Serves 4-6

Cucumber Salad

2 cucumbers, peeled, sliced (seeded if seeds are tough)
1/4 teaspoon salt
1 tomato, chopped, seeded
1 scallion, chopped
1/2 cup salad dressing
1/2 cup sour cream
1 1/2 Tablespoons apple cider vinegar
salt and pepper

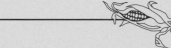

Place cucumbers and salt in a bowl and cover with water. Set aside. Combine remaining ingredients in a separate bowl. Drain cucumbers and stir in liquid. Add salt and fresh ground black pepper to taste.

This is an excellent sauce for wraps, or as a side salad.

Serves 4-6

29th August 1806
"I assended to the high Country and from an eminance, I had a view of the plains for a great distance. from this eminance I had a view of a greater number of buffalow than I had ever Seen before at one time. I must have Seen near 20,000 of those animals feeding on this plain."

William Clark

The Great Portage Baked Beans

1 pound Great Northern dry beans

1/2 teaspoon baking soda

1/2 medium onion, chopped

1 Tablespoon butter

1 Tablespoon salt

1/4 cup brown sugar

1/4 cup molasses

1/2 pound fresh pork or bacon

1/4 teaspoon liquid smoke

1 Tablespoon maple syrup

1/4 teaspoon fresh ground black pepper

Soak beans overnight. The next morning drain and cover with clean water. Par boil 1 hour, or until you can blow the skin off of the bean. Remove from heat. Add 1/2 teaspoon soda, stir, rinse and drain. In a skillet over medium-low heat, sauté onion in butter until translucent. Add beans, salt, sugar, molasses, meat, onion, liquid smoke, syrup, pepper and enough hot water to cover mixture. In crock or baking dish, bake at 350 degrees F. for 3 to 4 hours. Stir every hour after 2 hours. If beans seem dry add a little water and molasses mixture (1/4 cup of molasses to 1 quart of water).

Serves 6-8

Potato Salad

4 cups red potatoes, finely diced - should be about the size of a peanut

4 hardboiled eggs, peeled and diced to same size

1 Tablespoon onion, minced

1 stalk celery, sliced

salt and pepper to taste

Combine and let stand in refrigerator overnight

1 cup salad dressing
1/2 cup cream
1 teaspoon apple cider vinegar
1 teaspoon white granulated sugar
1 Tablespoon prepared mustard
dash salt
Combine and stir thoroughly. Mix with the potatoes.
Garnish with sliced boiled eggs, parsley and/or paprika.

Serves 6

Friday 27th December 1805

"In the evening Co-mo wool the Chief and 4 men of the Clat Sop nation they presented us a root which resembles the licquirish in Size and taste, which they roste like a potato which they call Cul ho-mo, also a black root which is cured in a kill like the pash-a-co above: this root has a Sweet taste and the natives are verry fond of it–"

William Clark

67

Hominy Croquettes

1 fifteen and a half-ounce can hominy, drained

2 Tablespoons milk

1 Tablespoon butter

1/4 teaspoon fresh ground black pepper

1/2 teaspoon parsley

1 scallion, chopped

2 eggs, beaten

2 cups dried bread crumbs

2 Tablespoons canola oil

Combine hominy, milk, butter, pepper, parsley, scallion and eggs in a saucepan over low heat, and stir until mixture is thick. Allow mixture to cool. Drop 1/4 cup mixture at a time in bread crumbs. Flip to bread both sides. Fry in hot oil and serve hot.

Garnish with paprika.

Serves 4

Sunday March 2nd 1806.

"The nativs of this neighbourhood eate the root of the Cattail or Cooper's flag. it is pleasantly tasted and appears to be very nutrecious."

William Clark

Cole Slaw

5 cups cabbage, finely shredded

1 cup salad dressing

3 teaspoons white granulated sugar

2 teaspoons vinegar

dash of salt

Shred the cabbage as finely as you can. In a bowl, combine salad dressing with sugar, vinegar and salt. Pour over cabbage and toss to coat. Raisins or currants may be added.

Serves 6

June 5th Tuesday 1804

"passed a Small Creek on L.S. opposit a Verry bad Sand bar of Several ms. in extent, which we named Sand C   here my Servent York Swam to the Sand bar to geather greens for our Dinner and returnd with a Sufficent quantity wild Creases [Cresses] or Teng [Tongue] grass,"

William Clark

Watercress Salad with Vinaigrette Dressing

Salad
1 bunch watercress, largest stems removed

4 scallions, chopped fine

4 cherry tomatoes, cut in half

4 red radishes, quartered

2 baby carrots, shredded

3 Tablespoons sunflower nuts, salted and roasted

Vinaigrette Dressing
1 Tablespoon apple cider vinegar

1/4 teaspoon salt

fresh ground black pepper to taste

1 clove garlic, minced

1 Tablespoon water

5 Tablespoons extra virgin olive oil

zest strips from one lemon

Layer all salad ingredients in a serving bowl. In a small mixing bowl, whisk together all the dressing ingredients except the oil and lemon zest. After the salt and sugar have dissolved, pour in the oil slowly, whisking constantly. Drizzle dressing over salad, tossing lightly.

Garnish with lemon zest and serve immediately.

Serves 4 as a side salad

Rocky Mountain Vegetable Roast

2 large carrots, cut into 4 inch lengths, quartered

3 medium potatoes, cut into wedges

2 medium mushrooms, sliced

1/2 green pepper, sliced

1 medium onion, sliced

1 tomato, cut into wedges

2 cloves garlic, minced

12 green olives

4 Tablespoons olive oil

1 Tablespoon seasoned rice vinegar

1/2 teaspoon salt

1/2 teaspoon dried oregano leaves

1/4 teaspoon fresh ground black pepper

1/8 teaspoon liquid smoke

Precook carrots and potatoes in microwave until tender. In a large bowl combine all the vegetables. In a separate bowl combine the oil, vinegar, spices and liquid smoke. Pour over vegetables and toss to coat. Marinate for about 30 minutes. Grill over hot coals in grill basket for 3 minutes each side. Transfer to serving dish.

Garnish with paprika and serve with sour cream

Serves 4

Mandan Roasted Corn Medley

10 ounces frozen corn

1/4 cup red bell pepper, diced

2 Tablespoons onion, diced

2 Tablespoons butter

1/3 cup Cheddar cheese, grated

Prepare corn according to package instructions. Drain off any liquid and in a pan, combine corn, pepper, onions, and butter. Sauté corn over medium heat until onion is translucent and corn becomes bright yellow (about ten minutes). Remove from heat. Sprinkle cheese on top and serve when cheese is melted.

Serves 3-4

Sunday April 7th 1805

"This Village lies on the South side of the River and contains 300 Lodges. the land adjoining it is Priaries, which gradually rise from the River, the Soil is very rich, producing Indian Corn, pumpkins, Squashes & beans in abundance"

Joseph Whitehouse

300. *Interior of a Mandan Earth Lodge*, watercolor and ink on paper, 11 ¼ X 16 ⅞

209. *Landscape with Herd of Buffalo on the Upper Missouri*, watercolor on paper, 9 5/8 X 12 3/8

Buffalo

Monday September 17th. 1804-
"this senery already rich pleasing and beatiful, was still farther
hightened by immence herds of Buffaloe deer Elk and Antelopes
which we saw in every direction feeding on the hills and plains. I do not
think I exagerate when I estimate the number of Buffaloe which could
be compreed at one view to amount to 3000."

Meriwether Lewis

Some Tips on Cooking Buffalo

The following tips are to help the first time cook. By following the tips you will enhance the flavor and moisture of the meat. It is important to remember that buffalo is a lean meat. This is one of the reasons for the gaining popularity of buffalo as an alternative to other red meats.

1. Never overcook buffalo. This dries the meat out and makes it tough. Buffalo cooks at a faster rate than beef. It needs to be watched. Low and slow is the rule of thumb.

2. Never use a fork when turning buffalo. Use tongs. If you poke the meat, this allows the juices to escape and you will have a dry piece of meat.

3. When marinating buffalo, try to use an oil based marinade. This allows the juices to be sealed inside.

4. When the buffalo is being grilled, do not use salt. This tends to dry the meat out. Salt the buffalo right before you take it off the grill.

5. When frying buffalo steaks, it is important to sear the meat at a high heat only to lock in the juices. Reduce the heat immediately and cook slowly.

6. When roasting, set your oven at 250 degrees to 275 degrees F. Basting every half hour helps the keep the meat moist.

7. Buffalo should be further from the heat source than beef, in most situations.

Mandan Buffalo Stew with Winter Squash

2 cups chicken stock

1 fifteen-ounce can tomato sauce

2 teaspoons garlic, minced

1 large onion, chopped

2 Tablespoons sun dried tomatoes in oil, minced

2 teaspoons extra virgin olive oil

1 pound cubed buffalo steak (substitute 3 chicken breasts)

1 teaspoon curry powder

1 teaspoon ground cumin

3/4 teaspoon ground cinnamon

2 cups peeled butternut or acorn squash, cut into 1-inch pieces

1 cup potatoes, peeled and diced

1/2 cup chopped spinach

1 cup corn

1/4 cup fresh cilantro, chopped

1 cup roasted, salted sunflower nuts

In a large Dutch oven combine chicken stock and tomato sauce. Bring to boil and reduce heat to a simmer. In a separate skillet over medium heat, sauté garlic, onions, and sun dried tomatoes in olive oil until onions are translucent. Add to liquid. Brown buffalo in same skillet (reduce heat and don't overcook). When buffalo is brown on all sides add to stew. Add spices, squash, potatoes, spinach, corn, and cilantro to stew. Simmer until squash is done.

Garnish with sunflower nuts.

Serves 6

Discovery Hash

Leftovers work best for this recipe.

2 cups cooked potatoes, grated

2 cups cooked buffalo, grated (substitute ground buffalo or beef)

1/2 cup onion, grated

salt and pepper to taste

1 cup fresh cooked corn, cut off the cob

1/4 cup butter

1/2 roasted salted sunflower nuts

gravy, if you have it

Combine potatoes, buffalo, onion and corn in skillet with melted butter. Salt and pepper to taste. Brown on medium heat.

Garnish with sunflower nuts and gravy.

Serves 4

Thursday April 25 1805

"the buffalo Elk and Antelope are so gentle that we pass near them while feeding, without apearing to excite any alarm among them, and when we attract their attention, they frequently approach us more nearly to discover what we are, and in some instances pursue us a considerable distance apparently with that view.—"

Meriwether Lewis

Marinated Buffalo Steaks

1 teaspoon ground ginger

3/4 Tablespoon rice vinegar

1 Tablespoon minced garlic

1 Tablespoon fresh ground black pepper

1/3 cup diced shallots

1/2 cup soy sauce

3/4 cup extra virgin olive oil

3/4 cup maple syrup

1 bay leaf

2 ten-ounce buffalo sirloin steaks (or beef sirloin tips)

Mix marinade in 1 gallon sealable plastic bag. Add meat. Make sure all meat is coated. Place bag in shallow pan. Marinate overnight in refrigerator. Turn bag at least once. Grill over hot coals to preference. (Remember, buffalo cooks about twice as fast as beef).

Serves 2

23 August Thursday 1804-

"J. Fields Sent out to hunt Came to the Boat and informed that he had killed a Buffalow in the plain a head. Capt. Lewis took 12 Men and had the buffalow brought to the boat in the next bend to the S.S."

William Clark

Cajun Buffalo Ribeye Steaks

Marinade

1/2 cup canola oil

2 dashes of hot pepper sauce

1/2 teaspoon liquid smoke

1 Tablespoon garlic, minced

1 onion, thinly sliced

1 Tablespoon plus 1/2 teaspoon fresh
   ground black pepper

2 Tablespoons soy sauce

4 sixteen-ounce ribeye buffalo steaks
   (or beef ribeye)

In a large sealable plastic bag, add oil, hot pepper sauce, liquid smoke, garlic, onion, pepper, soy sauce and steak. Make sure meat is well coated. Place bag in a shallow pan, turning at least once. Refrigerate overnight.

Spice Mixture

1 1/2 teaspoons ground paprika

1/2 teaspoon ground cayenne pepper

1/2 teaspoon salt

1/2 teaspoon fresh ground black pepper

1/8 teaspoon ground thyme

1/2 teaspoon dried basil leaves

2 Tablespoons butter

juice of 1/2 lemon

1/4 teaspoon salt

Remove steaks from marinade. Reserve marinade mixture. Sprinkle spice mixture on each side of steak and grill to preference. (Remember, buffalo cooks about twice as fast as beef). Drain oil from reserved marinade mixture and sauté with 2 tablespoons of butter, the juice of 1/2 lemon and 1/4 teaspoon of salt. Serve on the side.

Serves 4

Buffalo Skewers with Peanut Sauce

Marinade

1 Tablespoon soy sauce

3/4 teaspoon granulated white sugar

1/2 teaspoon dark sesame oil

1 Tablespoon ketchup

1/4 teaspoon fresh ground black pepper

1 1/2 Tablespoons extra virgin olive oil

1 Tablespoon corn starch

1 1/2 pounds of buffalo round steak sliced in thin strips, across the grain (substitute beef)

Peanut Sauce

1/4 cup of peanut butter, chunky

1/8 teaspoon ground cayenne pepper

1 Tablespoon water

1/2 Tablespoon ketchup

1 Tablespoon oyster sauce

1 clove garlic, minced

1/4 teaspoon ground ginger

1/2 teaspoon salt

Combine all the marinade ingredients and stir thoroughly. Pour over steak strips and marinate overnight in the refrigerator, turning at least once. If using wooden skewers, soak overnight in water or skewers will burn up on grill. Skewer the meat. Combine ingredients for peanut sauce in a bowl. Spread peanut sauce on the skewered meat. (Skewered meat can be stored this way in the refrigerator for up to 24 hours).

Grill over hot coals to preference. (Remember, buffalo cooks about twice as fast as beef).

Yield: 6 skewers

Buffalo Burgers

1 pound ground buffalo

1 egg, beaten

1 Tablespoon barbecue sauce

1 Tablespoon onion, minced

1/3 cup oatmeal

1/4 teaspoon salt

1/4 teaspoon fresh ground black pepper

1 teaspoon dried parsley

1 Tablespoon canola oil

Combine buffalo with egg, sauce, onion, oatmeal, salt, pepper, parsley and oil. Shape into 6 burgers. Grill on medium heat until patty is just brown. Flip and brown the other side. Do not overcook. May also be pan fried or broiled.

Yield: 6 burgers

Buffalo Strip Sauté

3/4 pound buffalo (or lean beef) round steak, cut into 1/4 inch thick strips

1 Tablespoon maple syrup

1 Tablespoon soy sauce

2 Tablespoons lemon juice

1/8 teaspoon hot pepper sauce

2 Tablespoons olive oil

3/4 cup onion, diced

3/4 cup green cabbage, sliced thin

1 medium carrot, sliced in thin rounds

1 rib celery, sliced on the diagonal

1 cup small cauliflower florets

1 Jerusalem artichoke, sliced

1 cup corn

1 clove garlic, minced

1-2 teaspoons soy sauce

1/2 teaspoon dried dill weed

1/4 teaspoon hot pepper sauce (optional)

Place the meat in a flat-bottomed (non-reactive) dish. In a bowl, whisk together the maple syrup, 1 Tablespoon soy sauce, lemon juice and 1/8-teaspoon hot pepper sauce. Pour the liquid over the meat, coating all pieces. Cover the dish and marinate in the refrigerator for at least 1 hour. Turn meat over once while marinating. In a large skillet over medium-low heat, add the oil, meat and any excess marinade. When the meat has started to brown add the onion, cabbage, carrot, celery, cauliflower, artichoke, corn and garlic. Stir well and sauté for 3-4 minutes. Add the soy sauce, dill weed and hot pepper sauce (if desired), sautéing until vegetables are tender. Remove from heat and cover. Allow flavors to blend for 5 minutes.

Serve with wild rice.

Serves 3-4

One Pot Stew with Cheese Dumplings

The Stew

1 cup onions, chopped

2 cloves garlic, minced

1 small zucchini, sliced thick

1 red bell pepper, julienne cut

1 pound ground buffalo (or lean ground beef)

2 cups of water

1/4 cup ketchup

1 teaspoon rice vinegar

1/2 teaspoon dried oregano leaves, crushed

1/4 teaspoon fresh ground black pepper

2 teaspoons beef base

3 medium potatoes, peeled, cubed

In a large dutch oven, over medium heat, sauté onions, garlic, zucchini, and red pepper. Add buffalo and brown. Add water, ketchup, vinegar, oregano, pepper, beef base and potatoes. Cover and simmer for 30 minutes.

The Cheese Dumplings

1/2 pound medium cheddar cheese, grated

2 cloves garlic, minced

1 teaspoon parsley

1/4 cup crumbled bacon bits

1/2 pound (2 sticks) butter, softened

2 cups flour

2 teaspoons baking powder

1/2 teaspoon ground cayenne pepper

1/4 teaspoon salt

3/4 cup milk or water, cold, as needed

Preheat oven to 350 degrees F. Mix grated cheese, garlic, parsley, bacon and butter in a bowl. Add flour, baking powder, pepper and salt. Mix well. Add only enough milk or water to form dough. Spoon biscuit batter on top of stew. Bake in oven for 30 minutes. A crust will form, sealing in stew.

Serve with cold dill pickles and a salad.

Serves 6

Sizzlin' Buffalo Breakfast Sausage

1 pound ground buffalo

1 pound ground pork

1 Tablespoon lemon juice

1 teaspoon black pepper

1 Tablespoon maple syrup

1 teaspoon salt

1/2 teaspoon cayenne pepper

1/8 teaspoon ground nutmeg

1/8 teaspoon ground allspice

1/4 teaspoon liquid smoke

1/2 cup beef jerky, ground fine

1/2 teaspoon roasted garlic, minced

Mix all ingredients together the night before and place in an air tight container in refrigerator. Form into patties 1/2-inch thick and fry over medium-low heat, turning frequently.

Serve with your favorite breakfast menu.

Yield: 10-15 patties

Thursday May 9th 1805

"we saw a great quantity of game today paricularly of Elk and Buffaloe, the latter are now so gentle that the men frequently throw sticks and stones at them in order to drive them out of the way."

Meriwether Lewis

Buffalo Sourdough Pizza

Crust

See recipe for **Sourdough Bread** in the Biscuit and Bread's Section on page 43.

For two pizzas: divide dough in half. Press onto cookie sheet to desired thickness. Poke with fork and let crust rest for 10 minutes. Arrange racks in oven to accommodate 2 cookie sheets. Preheat oven to 400 degrees F.

Sausage

See recipe for **Sizzlin' Buffalo Breakfast Sausage** in this section on page 85.

Crumble sausage into skillet and brown over medium-low heat. Remove from heat and drain fat. Prebake crust for 7 minutes. Remove from oven and turn oven up to 400 degrees F.

Topping

For each Pizza:

2 cups Mozzarella cheese, shredded (by placing the cheese first the dough resists moisture better)

1/2 green bell pepper, julienne cut

3 medium mushrooms, sliced

1 tomato, sliced

1/2 medium onion, julienne cut

1/2 of browned sausage

1 teaspoon dried oregano leaves

salt and fresh ground black pepper to taste

1/4 cup Parmesan cheese (more if desired)

Spread the cheese evenly over the warm crust. Return to oven until cheese is melted. Remove from oven. Layer remaining ingredients and return to oven for an additional 20-25 minutes, or until crust is brown. Remove from heat and drizzle with extra virgin olive oil and a little more Parmesan if desired.

Yield: 2 pizzas

Maple Marinated Buffalo Kabobs

3 pounds buffalo roast, English cut

1/2 cup canola oil

1/3 cup soy sauce

1/4 cup rice vinegar

2 Tablespoons prepared mustard

1 Tablespoon Worcestershire sauce

1 Tablespoon maple syrup

1/8 teaspoon cayenne pepper

Cut roast into quarters. Trim fat and membrane. Cut quarters into strips 1-inch wide and 1/4-inch thick. Add remaining marinade ingredients to a 1-gallon sealable plastic bag. Add buffalo strips to marinade bag. Place bag in a shallow tray, turning once. Marinate overnight in the refrigerator. If using wooden skewers, soak them in water overnight to prevent burning on the grill. Skewer kabobs with mushrooms and vegetables of your choice. Grill over medium heat to your preference. (Remember, buffalo cooks about twice as fast as beef).

Yield: 8 skewers

Thursday June 13th 1805

"my fare is really sumptuous this evening; buffaloe's humps, tongues and marrowbones, fine trout parched meal pepper and salt, and a good appetite; the last is not considered the least of the luxuries."

Meriwether Lewis

Roast Buffalo

1 three pound buffalo chuck roast

1 Tablespoon of canola oil

1 yellow onion, cut into rings, separated

2 bay leaves

2 cups water

In a large cast iron skillet, sear roast in hot oil. Place roast in crock pot with the rest of ingredients. Cook at least 8 hours on low. *Alternate method:* Place in covered roasting pan and bake at 250 degrees F until tender (at least 4 hours).

Serve with your favorite potatoes.

Serves 4-6

Sunday, September 16th, 1804.
vast herds of Buffaloe deer Elk and Antilopes were seen feeding in every direction as far as the eye of the observer could reach.

Meriwether Lewis

Stuffed Buffalo Tenderloin with Smoked Gouda Relish

Stuffing

1 shallot, minced
1 Tablespoon Parmesan cheese, grated
4 teaspoons sourdough bread crumbs
1 Tablespoon extra virgin olive oil
1 Tablespoon sundried tomatoes, minced
4 mushrooms, small dice
2 buffalo tenderloins

Combine all ingredients except the meat, in a small bowl. Butterfly the meat and spoon in stuffing. Tie up each steak with kitchen string. Broil steaks to preference. (Remember, to broil further away from broiler and buffalo cooks in about half the time beef does).

Relish

1/2 cup smoked Gouda cheese, small dice
1 Tablespoon fresh chives, minced
1 small tomato, seeded, small dice
1 Tablespoon extra virgin olive oil
1 Tablespoon apple cider vinegar
salt and pepper to taste

Combine all ingredients in a bowl and toss lightly. Marinate in refrigerator. After cutting off the strings, spoon over top of meat and serve immediately.

Serve with baked potato and your favorite salad.

Serves 2

Hitdatsa Buffalo Stew

Sauce

1/4 cup molasses
1/2 Tablespoon black peppercorns, crushed
4 whole star anise
2 1/2 Tablespoons Szechuan sweet bean sauce
4 Tablespoons soy sauce
1/4 cup raisins, diced fine
5 teaspoons Szechuan chili bean sauce

Combine all ingredients in a small bowl.

Stew

1 Tablespoon fresh ginger, minced
1/4 cup scallions, chopped
2 cloves of garlic, minced and pressed
2 Tablespoons extra virgin olive oil
2 pounds buffalo stew meat, 1/2-inch cubes
3 cups of water
1 cup of corn
1/2 cup roasted, salted sunflower nuts
2 cups cooked butternut squash
2 cups carrots, sliced

In a large dutch oven saute ginger, scallions and garlic in oil over medium heat. Add meat to dutch oven and brown slightly. Add 3 cups water, corn, sunflower nuts, squash, carrots and sauce mixture. Reduce heat, cover and simmer for 1 hour stirring occasionally.

Serves 6

316. *Síh-Chilä, Mandan Man,* watercolor on paper, 17 1/8 X 11 7/8

205. *Blackfeet-Assiniboin Girl,* watercolor on paper, 10 ⁵/₈ X 8

Elk & Venison

July 27, 1806

"The Buffalow and Elk is estonishingly noumerous on the banks of the river on each Side, particularly the Elk which lay on almost every point in large gang and are So jintle that we frequently pass within 20 or 30 paces of them without their being the least alarmd."

William Clark

Elk Stroganoff and Strudels

Strudel

1 1/2 cups lukewarm water

1 teaspoon salt

1 egg, beaten

1 Tablespoon extra virgin olive oil

1 teaspoon yeast with 1/2 teaspoon granulated white sugar

4 1/2 cups of sifted all-purpose white flour (start with 3 and knead in remainder as needed)

3 Tablespoons butter, softened

Combine ingredients in a large bowl. Knead until smooth. Let rise in a warm place for 30 minutes. Divide dough into fourths. For each piece of dough, roll out on a slightly buttered surface to 1/2-inch thickness. Spread dough with butter and let rise for 10 minutes. Stretch each rolled dough so thin you can see through it. Roll loosely, cut in 4 inch lengths and let rest for 1/2 hour.

1 pound of elk sirloin cut into bite size pieces (substitute buffalo or beef)

Sifted all-purpose white flour for dredging

Olive oil and butter for browning

Salt

Fresh ground black pepper

1/4 cup chopped onion

1/4 cup mushrooms, sliced

1 clove garlic, minced

1 Tablespoon ketchup

1 cup beef stock

1 Tablespoon sifted all purpose white flour

1 cup sour cream

Preheat oven to 325 degrees F. Dredge meat in flour and brown in oil and butter. Add salt, pepper, onions, mushrooms and garlic. Sauté until onions are translucent. Add ketchup, beef stock and flour, stir well. Place strudels in kettle over meat and bake for 45 minutes. (Don't lift cover). Place strudels on warm serving plate. Add cream to kettle and stir to loosen drippings. Pour over strudels and serve.

Serves 6

Wild Raspberry Venison Stew

2 pounds venison stew meat (or beef) in chunks

1/2 cup sifted all-purpose white flour, seasoned with salt and fresh ground black pepper

2 Tablespoons extra virgin olive oil

2 Tablespoons butter

1 clove garlic, minced

1 cup onions, chopped

1 cup carrots, diced

1 cup celery, sliced

1/2 cup white grape juice

1 cup of water

juice from 1 lemon

1 Tablespoon lemon zest

1 teaspoon apple cider vinegar

1/4 cup maple syrup

2 teaspoons chicken bouillon

3 Tablespoons wild raspberry jam

1 cup fresh mushrooms, chopped

Dredge meat in flour and brown in oil and butter. Remove meat from kettle and set aside. Add garlic, onions, carrots and celery to kettle and sauté until onions are translucent. Add grape juice, water, lemon juice, lemon zest, vinegar, syrup, bouillon, jam and mushrooms. Simmer for 10 minutes. Return meat to kettle and simmer an additional 10 minutes.

Serve over rice.

Serves 4-6

June 10th Sunday 1804

"Camped in a Prarie on the L.S., Capt Lewis & my self Walked out 3 ms. found the Country roleing open & rich, with plenty of water, great qts of Deer"

William Clark

95

The Bleú Stag

1 pound venison sirloin steak, tenderized, (or beef ribeye)

1 Tablespoon olive oil

2 Tablespoons Bleú cheese

2 Tablespoons sour cream

1 teaspoon Worcestershire sauce

1 clove garlic, minced

1/4 teaspoon hot pepper sauce

3 drops liquid smoke

1 Tablespoon fresh tarragon, chopped

salt and pepper to taste

Preheat oven to 350 degrees F. Brown steak in olive oil. Combine remaining ingredients in a bowl and stir until smooth. When the meat is browned on both sides, cover with the cheese mixture and bake in the oven for 15-20 minutes.

Serve with your favorite bread and salad.

Serves 2-3

Sunday June 24th 1804

"emince number of Deer on both Sides of the river, we pass between two Sand bars at head of which we had to raise the boat 8 Inch to get her over, Camped at the Lower point of a Isd. on the L.S. the Party in high Spirits."

Lewis and Clark

Venison Swiss Steak

1 pound venison round or tenderloin
(or beef round steak), tenderized

salt and fresh ground black pepper

sifted all-purpose white flour for
dredging

1 Tablespoon butter

1 Tablespoon extra virgin olive oil

1 scallion, chopped

1 large portabella mushroom

2 cloves garlic, minced

1 teaspoon Worcestershire sauce

1 1/2 cups cream

1 Tablespoon Bleú cheese

Preheat oven to 350 degrees F. Salt and pepper steaks. Dredge steaks in flour and brown in oil and butter. Place steaks in roaster. Sauté scallion, mushrooms, and garlic until scallion is translucent. Stir in Worcestershire sauce, cream, cheese and salt and pepper. Stir until cheese melts. Pour over steaks and bake for 30 minutes.

Serve with potatoes.

Serves 4

Saturday July 13 th, 1805

"we eat an emensity of meat; it requires 4 deer, an Elk and a deer, or one buffaloe, to supply us plentifully 24 hours. meat now forms our food prinsipally as we reserve our flour parched meal and corn as much as possible for the rocky mountains which we are shortly to enter, and where from the indian account game is not very abundant."

Meriwether Lewis

Savory Mustard Venison

1 pound venison, round steak (or beef round steak)
   trimmed and tenderized, cut into strips

1/3 cup prepared mustard

1/2 teaspoon granulated white sugar

1/2 teaspoon fresh ground pepper

sifted all-purpose white flour for dredging

butter for frying

Combine mustard, sugar and pepper. Spread on meat and refrigerate for at least one hour. Dredge meat in flour and brown in butter.

Serve with your favorite bread and salad.

Serves 2

30th June 1804

"Deer to be Seen in every direction and their tracks ar as plenty as Hogs about a farm,"

William Clark

Venison Stew

1 teaspoon garlic, minced

1 large onion, chopped

2 stalks celery, sliced on the diagonal

2 Tablespoons butter

2 large carrots, sliced

4 medium potatoes, cubed

2 cups of water

1/2 teaspoon salt

1 Tablespoon chicken flavored granules

1 package mushroom gravy

1 cup shredded cabbage

1/2 cup mushrooms, chopped

2 Tablespoons fresh cilantro chopped

1/2 teaspoon seasoned salt

1/2 teaspoon dried oregano leaves

1/8 teaspoon ground cloves

2 fresh tomatoes, chopped

1/2 cup corn kernels

1 1/2 pounds venison round steak, sliced (across the grain)

1 1/2 cups of sifted all-purpose white flour

2 Tablespoons butter

In a large kettle, sauté garlic, onion and celery in butter until onions are translucent. Add carrots, potatoes, water, salt, and chicken granules. Simmer until carrots are tender. Add remaining ingredients except the venison, flour and butter. Add butter to a large skillet over medium-low heat. Dredge venison in flour and place in hot butter. Sauté until brown. Set aside. Add meat to stew when carrots are tender. Simmer an additional 5 minutes.

Garnish with a dab of sour cream and parsley.

Serves 6

Venison Jerky

3 pounds ground venison, (or lean beef)
2 Tablespoons tenderizing salt
1 teaspoon garlic, minced
1 1/2 teaspoons onion, minced
1 Tablespoon water
1 1/2 teaspoons hickory smoked salt
1 teaspoon black pepper, coarsely ground
2 teaspoons liquid smoke
1 teaspoon ground paprika
1 Tablespoon maple syrup

In a large bowl, combine venison and tenderizing salt. In small bowl combine garlic, onion and water. Microwave on low until onion is translucent. Let onion mixture cool, then strain into meat mixture. Add remaining ingredients. Mix well and let stand for 1 hour. Line a cookie sheet with waxed paper. Press venison onto paper. Top with waxed paper. Roll with rolling pin to flatten meat mixture to 1/4 inch thick. Freeze meat mixture slightly (about 30 minutes). Remove top wax paper and cut meat into strips. Dry in dehydrator or in oven at about 180 degrees F. If you prefer a moister, chewier jerky, roll jerky out a little thicker and do not over dry. Drying time is approximately 8 hours.

Yield: about 80 4-inch strips

August the 1st 1804

"This being my birth day I order'd a Saddle of fat Vennison, an Elk fleece & a Bevertail to be cooked and a Desert of Cheries, Plumbs, Raspberries Currents and grapes of a Supr. quallity."

William Clark

Venison Shepherd's Pie

1 Tablespoon canola oil

1 pound ground venison (substitute buffalo or lean beef)

1/2 cup onion, chopped

1 rib celery, diced

1 medium ripe tomato, chopped

1 small carrot, grated

1 Tablespoon ketchup

1 Tablespoon prepared mustard

1 teaspoon Worcestershire sauce

salt and fresh ground black pepper to taste

3 Tablespoons grated Parmesan cheese

2-3 cups cooked, mashed potatoes

butter

paprika

Preheat oven to 325 degrees F. Pour the oil into a large skillet over medium low heat. Brown the venison, breaking up any larger pieces. Add the onion, celery, tomato and carrot; sautéing for 2-3 minutes. Stir in the ketchup, mustard and Worcestershire sauce. Salt and pepper to taste. Add the Parmesan cheese and transfer the mixture to an oiled baking dish, spreading evenly with a spatula. Spread the mashed potatoes evenly over the mixture and dot the top with butter. Bake for 20-25 minutes. Remove from heat and sprinkle with paprika and additional salt and pepper if desired.

Serves 3-5

Venison Chili

1 pound ground venison (or lean beef)

2 Tablespoons canola oil

2 small white onions, chopped fine

1 fresh jalapeno pepper, seeded and diced

2 cloves garlic, minced

salt and pepper

1 Tablespoon chili powder

3/4 teaspoon dried cumin seed

2-3 cups tomato juice

In a large heavy skillet over medium low heat, brown the meat in the oil; breaking up any large pieces. When the meat is partially browned, add the onions, jalapeno pepper and garlic. Salt and pepper to taste. Sauté for 3-4 minutes, stirring constantly. Add the chili powder and cumin seed. Sauté an additional 3-5 minutes, adding small amounts of the tomato juice if needed. Now add the 2-3 cups of tomato juice. Simmer for 30 minutes, stirring occasionally. Remove from heat, cover and allow flavors to blend for 10 minutes.

Garnish with your choice of fresh salsa, grated Cheddar cheese, sour cream, minced scallions or cilantro.

Serve with biscuits or cornbread and a salad.

Serves 3-5

Venison Pepper Steak

2 Tablespoons canola oil

1 pound venison steak (substitute beef), cut into 1/4-inch strips

1 large yellow onion, peeled, cut into 12 sections

1 green bell pepper, seeded, cut into 8 sections

1 red bell pepper, seeded, cut into 8 sections

1/4 teaspoon ground cumin (optional)

salt and fresh ground black pepper

2-3 Tablespoons soy sauce

sesame seeds

chopped scallions

Pour the oil into a heavy skillet over medium-low heat. When the oil is hot, add the venison strips and brown them, stirring occasionally. Add the onion, peppers and cumin, if desired. Stir constantly for 1 minute and add salt and pepper to taste. Sauté for an additional 2-3 minutes and add the soy sauce. Cover and simmer for 10-15 minutes, until venison is tender. Serve with rice.

Garnish with sesame seeds and scallions.

Serves 3

Elk with Chokecherry Sauce

2 pounds elk or venison chops

sifted all-purpose white flour
    for dredging

1 Tablespoon butter

1 Tablespoon canola oil

salt and pepper

1 package onion soup mix

1/4 cup maple syrup

1 cup chokecherry jelly (grape may be
    substituted)

1/2 cup western salad dressing

1 cup brown sugar, packed

1 Tablespoon apple cider vinegar

1/2 green bell pepper, cut in large
    chunks

Dredge chops in flour, brown in butter and oil over medium heat in large skillet until done (about 8 minutes each side). Remove to warming plate. Combine soup mix, syrup, jelly, dressing, sugar and vinegar in same browning skillet. Stir drippings over medium heat until sauce is hot and well blended. Stir in bell pepper and remove from heat. Let flavors mingle for about 5 minutes. Pour sauce over chops and serve.

Serves 6

Monday August 26th 1805

"I directed the hunters to turn out early in the morning and indeavor to obtain some meat. I had nothing but a little parched corn to eat this evening."

Meriwether Lewis

Venison Steak with Cranberry Sauce

1 cup chicken broth

1 cup beef broth

1/4 cup maple syrup

1/3 cup dried cranberries

1 pound venison steak, salted,
    peppered, tenderized

3 Tablespoons butter

1 scallion, chopped

1 teaspoon raspberry jam

1 Tablespoon plus 1 teaspoon apple
    cider vinegar

Combine broths, syrup and cranberries in saucepan. Heat to slow boil until sauce is reduced by half. Fry tenderized, seasoned steak in butter. Remove steaks to warming plate. Deglaze the steak pan with sauce. Add scallions, jam and vinegar. Stir and reheat.

Serves 2

August 1st 1805

"I felt my sperits much revived on our near approach to the river at the sight of a herd of Elk of which Drewyer and myself killed two. we then hurried to the river and allayed our thirst. I ordered two of the men to skin the Elk and bring the meat to the river while myself and the other prepared a fire and cooked some of the meat for our dinner. we made a comfortable meal of the Elk and left the ballance of the meat on the bank of the river the party with Capt. Clark. this supply was no doubt very acceptable to them as they had had no fresh meat for near two days except one beaver Game being very scarce and shy."

Meriwether Lewis

105

Venison Breakfast Sausage

1 pound ground venison

1/2 pound fresh ground pork

1 Tablespoon roasted garlic, minced

1 Tablespoon maple syrup

1 Tablespoon apple cider vinegar

1 Tablespoon canola oil

2 teaspoons fresh ground black pepper

1 1/4 teaspoons salt

1/2 teaspoon ground nutmeg

1/4 teaspoon ground cloves

1/4 teaspoon ground cumin

1/4 teaspoon ground cayenne pepper

1/8 teaspoon liquid smoke

Combine all of the ingredients and refrigerate overnight to allow the flavors to mingle. Shape into patties. Fry and serve with your favorite morning entrées.

Yield: 9-12 sausage patties

Elk and Pork Meat Balls

1 pound ground elk

1 pound ground pork

1/3 cup onions, chopped

1 teaspoon garlic, minced

1/4 teaspoon fresh ground black pepper

1/4 cup green salad olives

1/4 cup Bleú cheese, crumbled

1/2 teaspoon salt

1 egg, beaten

1/3 cup oatmeal

1 Tablespoon canola oil

1 Tablespoon butter

1 package brown gravy mix

1/4 cup onions, chopped

3 medium mushrooms, sliced

2 Tablespoons butter

1/4 teaspoon seasoned salt

1/2 cup sour cream

In a medium bowl, combine elk, pork, onions, garlic, pepper, olives, Bleú cheese, salt, egg, and oatmeal. Cover bowl and refrigerate overnight. Next day, shape into meatballs. Brown in butter and oil. Remove meatballs and place on plate. Prepare gravy-mix according to package instructions. Return meatballs to gravy. In small pan, sauté onions and mushrooms in butter until onions are translucent. Stir onion/mushroom mixture and seasoned salt in with the gravy. Reheat meatballs over medium-low heat for 10 minutes. Stir in 1/2 cup sour cream and serve.

Serves 6

Monday August 12th 1805

"I now decended the mountain about 3/4 of a mile which I found much steeper than on the opposite side, to a handsome bold running Creek of cold Clear water. here I first tasted the water of the great Columbia river."

Meriwether Lewis

Venison with Chokecherry Sauce

<u>Sauce:</u>

2 Tablespoons chokecherry jelly (or grape jelly)

1 Tablespoon apple cider vinegar

1 teaspoon soy sauce

1/4 teaspoon fresh ground ginger

2 teaspoons corn starch

Combine all ingredients in a saucepan. Bring to a boil stirring constantly until jelly is melted. Remove from heat.

<u>Meat:</u>

1 pound venison round steak, tenderized,
    fat trimmed and cut into 6 ounce serving sizes

salt and fresh ground black pepper

sifted all-purpose white flour for dredging (about 1/3 cup)

1 Tablespoon extra virgin olive oil

Salt and pepper tenderized steak. Dredge in flour. In a large skillet fry steak in butter and oil until golden brown. Turn and brown the other side. Pour sauce over meat.

Serve with rice.

Garnish with chopped scallions.

Serves 3

195. *Junction of the Yellowstone and the Missouri,* watercolor on paper, 10 3/8 X 16 3/4

270. *View of the Bear Paw Mountains from Fort McKenzie*, watercolor on paper, 11 ½ X 16 ³/₈

Fish and Fowl

October 17th Thursday 1805

"I was furnished with a mat to Sit on, and one man Set about prepareing me Something to eate, first he brought in a piece of Drift log of pine and with a wedge of the elks horn, and a malet of Stone curioesly Carved he Split the log into Small pieces and lay'd it open on the fire on which he put round Stones, a woman handed him a basket of water a large Salmon about half Dried, when the Stones were hot he put them into the basket of water with the fish which was Soon Sufficently boiled for use. it was then taken out put on a platter of rushes neetly made, and Set before me they boiled a Salmon for each of the men with me, dureing those preperations, I Smoked with those about me who Chose to Smoke which was but fiew, this being a custom those people are but little accustomed to and only Smok thro form. after eateing the boiled fish which was delcious, I Set out...."

William Clark

Cajun Catfish Chowder

*1 pound catfish fillets, blanched and
   cut into chunks

3 slices bacon

1 teaspoon garlic, minced

1 cup onion, chopped

1 stalk of celery, chopped

2 Tablespoons of butter

3 small potatoes, cubed

2 tomatoes, diced

1 carrot, sliced

2 cups water (reserved)

2 cups corn kernels

2 teaspoons dried parsley flakes

1/2 teaspoon dried oregano

1/4 teaspoon salt (optional)

Fresh ground black pepper, to taste

1 Tablespoon Cajun seafood seasoning

2 teaspoons dried thyme

1 pint heavy cream

*Blanching the catfish firms the flesh. Bring a large kettle of water to a rolling boil.
Drop fillets into boiling water, one at a time. Leave in for about 30-45 seconds,
remove from water and set aside. Reserve 2 cups of the water.

Fry bacon on low heat until crisp in a large soup pot. Drain bacon on paper towels.
Crumble. Drain bacon grease and sauté garlic, onions and celery in butter until
tender in same pot. Add potatoes, tomatoes, and reserved 2 cups water. Cover and
simmer until potatoes are tender. Add the remaining ingredients (except cream and
catfish) and simmer 5 minutes, stirring occasionally. Add the cream and catfish.
Adjust seasonings, if desired. Simmer another 5-10 minutes. Do not allow chowder
to boil. Remove from heat and allow flavors to blend about 10 minutes.

Garnish with crumbled bacon pieces.

Serves 3-5

Pacific and Columbia Lasagna

Sauce

1/3 cup butter

1 shallot, chopped

1 Tablespoon garlic, minced

1/3 cup sifted all-purpose white flour

2 six and a half-ounce cans of chopped
   clams, including the juice

1 cup of whole milk

2 cups cream

1 cup smoked Gouda cheese, grated

1/4 cup Parmesan cheese, grated

1/2 cup Cheddar cheese, grated

3/4 teaspoon dried thyme

1/2 teaspoon dried oregano leaves

1/2 teaspoon dried dill weed

1/8 teaspoon liquid smoke

Sauté shallot and garlic in butter until shallot is translucent. Stir in flour and mix until a paste is formed. Stir in clams, milk, and cream. When smooth, add Gouda, Parmesan and Cheddar. Add spices and liquid smoke. Stir constantly until cheese is melted. Turn off heat and set aside.

Lasagna

9 Lasagna noodles, cooked and cooled

1 cup smoked salmon, flaked and
   deboned

2 1/2 cups spinach, chopped and well
   drained

2 small tomatoes, diced

1/2 pound shrimp, deveined, peeled

1/2 cup Parmesan cheese, grated

Preheat oven to 350 degrees F. Butter a 9x13-inch baking pan. Put a little sauce in bottom of pan. Arrange 3 noodles on bottom. Spoon a little sauce on noodles. Evenly distribute salmon. Next, layer 3 more noodles and top with spinach, tomatoes, and 1/2 of the remaining sauce. Sprinkle 1/4 cup Parmesan cheese on top of that and then place the last layer of noodles. Arrange shrimp, remaining sauce and add remaining Parmesan cheese. Cover with foil and bake for 40 minutes. Remove foil and bake an additional 10 minutes. Remove from oven and allow to set for 15 minutes. Cut into squares. Garnish with fresh parsley.

Yield: 9 squares

Stovetop Pheasant

2-3 Tablespoons canola oil

1 pheasant (or chicken) cut up and deboned

Sifted all-purpose white flour for dredging, seasoned with salt, pepper and paprika

1 medium onion, diced

1 green bell pepper, julienne cut

2 cloves garlic, minced

1 fourteen and one half-ounce can stewed tomatoes, crushed, with juice

fresh basil, chopped scallions and grated Parmesan cheese

Pour oil into a heavy skillet over medium-low heat. When the oil is hot, begin dredging the meat in the seasoned flour. Shake off the extra flour from each piece. Brown meat on both sides and remove from skillet. Add onion, bell pepper and garlic to skillet. Salt and pepper to taste. Sauté for about 5 minutes and then stir in the tomatoes. Sauté for about 3 minutes, stirring constantly. Return the pheasant to the skillet, reduce heat to simmer; cover and cook until pheasant is done (about 15-20 minutes).

Garnish with basil, scallions and Parmesan.

Serves 3-4

July 29th Sunday 1804

"Cought three large Cat fish to day verry fat one of them nearly white those Cat are So plenty that they may be Cought in any part of this river but few fish of any other Kind.—"

William Clark

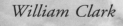

Pan Blackened Salmon

1 teaspoon salt

1/4 teaspoon dried thyme

1/2 teaspoon onion powder

1/2 teaspoon dried oregano leaves

1/2 teaspoon ground cayenne pepper

1 teaspoon sweet paprika

1/2 teaspoon garlic powder

1/2 teaspoon fresh ground black pepper

2 Tablespoons butter, melted

4 six-ounce salmon steaks

8 teaspoons butter, melted

Combine spices in a small bowl. Pat salmon steaks dry. Dip steaks in 2 Tablespoons melted butter, then sprinkle spices on each side. Heat cast iron skillet on high outdoors until it quits smoking (about 8 minutes). Place steaks (one at a time) in the hot skillet. Pour 1 teaspoon of butter on the fillet. Butter may flare up. After 2 minutes, turn, pour 1 teaspoon of butter on steak and fry an additional 2 minutes. Remove and repeat process with the rest of the steaks.

Serve with Hollandaise Sauce, (see **Marinades and Sauces**, page 143).

Serves 4

Aug 16th 1804

"...Capt Lewis with [12] men went out to the Creek & Pond & Caught about 800 fine fish with Bush Drag..."

William Clark

115

Portabella Crab and Cheese Bake

The Crust:
3 Tablespoons butter, melted

1/2 cup Parmesan cheese, grated

1 cup sourdough breadcrumbs

Preheat oven to 350 degrees F. Combine sourdough crumbs, cheese and butter in bottom of pie pan. Bake 15 minutes until crust is light brown. Remove and cool.

The Filling:

1/2 Tablespoon extra virgin olive oil

1/2 cup onion, chopped

2 teaspoons garlic, minced

1/2 cup red bell pepper, minced

2 cups portabella mushrooms, coarsely chopped

2 eight-ounce packages cream cheese, softened

1 teaspoon seafood seasoning

1/2 teaspoon fresh ground black pepper

2 large eggs, beaten

1/4 cup whipping cream

5 ounces crabmeat, shredded

1/2 cup smoked Gouda cheese, grated

1 teaspoon chives, minced

Sauté onion, garlic, pepper and mushrooms in olive oil until onions are translucent. Remove from heat and set aside. In a medium bowl combine the cheese with the seasonings. Stir in the eggs and cream. Add crabmeat, Gouda, chives and sautéd onion mixture. Stir to combine, pour over crust. Bake for 1 hour until top is slightly brown. Cool for 1 hour.

Serve in wedges.

Serves 8

Smoked Oyster Stew

3 eight-ounce cans of oysters in liquid

2 3.75-ounce tins smoked oysters, drained

1/2 pound American cheese cubed

1 pint heavy cream

1 eight-ounce package cream cheese

1 teaspoon of liquid smoke

In a large crock pot add all ingredients. Set heat on high and cook until cheese is melted. Stir to blend. Serve hot.

Garnish with oyster crackers.

Serves 6

Monday August 19th 1805

"the trout are the same which I first met with at the falls of the Missouri, they are larger than the speckled trout of our mountains and equally as well favored.—"

Meriwether Lewis

Crab Stew

1 teaspoon garlic, minced

2 onions chopped

2 stalks celery, sliced

1 Tablespoon butter

4 large carrots, sliced

2 cups chicken broth

2 bay leaves

3/4 teaspoon dried thyme, crumbled

1/2 cup packed fresh parsley, washed and dried

1/4 teaspoon whole black peppercorns

1 fifteen-ounce can tomato sauce

2 teaspoons seafood seasoning

1 teaspoon fresh dill weed (minced fine)

1 teaspoon lemon zest

juice of 1/2 lemon

1 pound crab meat or mock crab

1 cup cream

In a large skillet, sauté garlic, onions and celery in butter until onions are translucent. Add carrots, broth, bay leaves, thyme, parsley, peppercorns, tomato sauce, seafood seasoning, dill weed, lemon zest, and lemon juice. Simmer until carrots are tender. Add crab and cream and simmer for 5 minutes. Do not boil. Discard bay leaves.

Garnish with fresh chives.

Serves 6

October 26th Saturday 1805

"one of the guard at the river guiged a Salmon Trout, which we had fried in a little Bears Oil which a Chief we passed below the narrows gave us: [thought this]this | thought one of the most delicious fish | have ever tasted"

William Clark

Walleye Chowder

1 pound fresh walleye
2 eight-ounce bottles of clam juice
2 eight-ounce cans of clams
1/2 teaspoon dried thyme
1/2 teaspoon dry mustard
1/2 teaspoon dried dill weed
1 Tablespoon lemon zest
1 pound of pepper bacon, cubed
2 cloves garlic, minced
1 medium onion, chopped
2 stalks celery, sliced diagonally
2 Tablespoons butter

2 cups water
2 bay leaves
2 large potatoes, peeled and diced
1 carrot, diced
3/4 teaspoon salt
1/2 teaspoon fresh ground black pepper
1/2 cup frozen spinach, chopped and
    drained
1 cup cooked wild rice
4 cups cream
1 cup scallions, chopped
Paprika

Place the walleye, clam juice, juice from cans of clams, thyme, dry mustard, dill and lemon zest in large skillet. Turn on heat and bring up slowly. Don't boil the fish or it will toughen the flesh. Simmer until done, about 8 minutes. Pour stock into a bowl. Let fish cool on plate. Remove skin and bones. Flake the fish. Place bacon in skillet over medium-low heat and fry slowly until crisp. Discard fat and drain bacon on paper towels. Crumble bacon into bits after it has cooled. Add the garlic, onions, celery, and butter to the same skillet and sauté until onions are translucent. In a large soup kettle place the garlic mixture, water, bay leaves, potatoes, carrots, clams, salt, and pepper. Add 2 cups of the poaching broth, (add more clam juice if needed). Bring heat up gradually to a light boil. Reduce heat and simmer for about 15 minutes, until potatoes are tender. Add fish, chopped spinach, and wild rice. Stir in cream gradually until blended. Do not boil after this point. Stir gently. Remove from heat and let stand for 30 minute for the flavors to blend. Discard bay leaves. Gently reheat if necessary.

Garnish with bacon, scallions and a dash of paprika.

Serves 5-8

Virginia Clam Chowder

1 eight-ounce bottle of clam juice

1 cup water

1/2 teaspoon caraway seed

3 to 4 crushed black peppercorns

1 bay leaf

1 whole clove

1/4 teaspoon dried thyme

1 cup chicken broth

2 six and a half-ounce cans of clams

1 cup chopped onions

1 teaspoon roasted garlic

1 cup chopped celery

4 ounces of smoked sausage, diced fine

1/4 pound butter (1 stick)

1/2 cup sifted all-purpose white flour

2 cups cooked potatoes, peeled and diced

1 large carrot, grated

1 pint of milk

1 cup of cream

Colby cheese

fresh dill weed

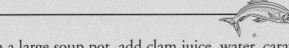

In a large soup pot, add clam juice, water, caraway, peppercorns, bay leaf, clove, thyme and chicken broth. Turn heat up slowly until broth reaches a light boil. Reduce heat and simmer for 20 minutes stirring occasionally. Strain broth into a large bowl, discard contents of strainer, return broth to stock pot and resume simmering. Add clams while stock is simmering. Sauté onion, garlic, celery and diced sausage in butter in a large skillet. Cook until the onion is tender yet firm. Add the flour to the skillet mixture, stirring constantly. Take about a cup of broth from the soup pot and gradually add it to the skillet mixture, stirring constantly to make a thickening. Add thickening to soup pot and stir. Add potatoes, carrots, milk and cream. Simmer for 20 minutes or until potatoes are tender. Do not boil. Remove from heat and cover. Let stand for 20 minutes.

Garnish with a little grated Colby cheese and fresh dill weed.

Serves 3-5

Ribald Manhattan Style Clam Chowder

1 1/2 pounds skinless halibut fillets

4 slices smoked Canadian style bacon, chopped

1 Tablespoon butter

3 garlic cloves, minced

1 cup onions, chopped

1 cup celery, chopped

1 bay leaf

1/2 teaspoon ground thyme

1 four and a half-ounce can diced green chilies

1 eight-ounce bottle clam juice

2 sixteen-ounce cans of stewed tomatoes

1 large potato, peeled and diced

1 sixteen-ounce jar salsa

2 six and one half-ounce cans chopped clams, with liquid

1 cup fresh cilantro leaves, chopped, lightly packed

Parmesan cheese

Place halibut fillets on broiler pan and broil until done, approximately 10 minutes. Allow to cool, then debone and tear into bite size pieces. Set aside. In a large skillet, fry bacon until brown. Transfer bacon to large soup kettle. Add butter, garlic, onions, celery, bay leaf and thyme. Cook until onions are translucent but still firm. Add chilies, clam juice, tomatoes and potato. Bring to a rolling boil, then reduce to simmer. Cook until potatoes are tender. Add halibut, salsa and clams with all of their juices. Simmer an additional 5 minutes. Stir in Cilantro and serve.

Garnish with grated Parmesan cheese.

Serves 4-6

Smoked Salmon Chowder

1 Tablespoon butter

1 small onion, diced fine

1 pound smoked salmon

4 medium potatoes, peeled and diced

1 carrot, grated

2 cups water, salted

1/2 teaspoon liquid smoke

1/4 pound American cheese, large grate

1 1/2 cups whole kernel corn

1 Tablespoon Bleú cheese, crumbled

1 cup heavy cream

1 carrot, large grate

In a skillet, sauté onions in butter until translucent. Remove the skin, debone and flake the salmon. In a soup pot, cook potatoes and carrots in 2 cups of salted water until tender. Add remaining ingredients. Simmer for 30 minutes, stirring occasionally. Do not allow the chowder to boil. Serve hot.

Garnish with fresh ground black pepper and fresh minced chives.

Serves 4-6

December 9th Monday 1805

"...those people treated me with extrodeanary friendship, one man attached himself to me as Soon as I entered the hut, Spred down new mats for me to Set on, gave me fish berries rutes &c. on Small neet platteers of rushes to eate which was repeated, all the Men of the other houses Came and Smoked with me..."

William Clark

Skillet Shrimp and Potatoes

2 Tablespoons olive oil

2 Tablespoons butter

2 medium white onions, diced

2 cloves garlic, minced

10 baby carrots, cut in 3 pieces each

3 medium potatoes, peeled, 1/2-inch dice

1/2 teaspoon dried dill weed

salt and fresh ground black pepper to taste

1 pound medium shrimp, peeled and deveined

the juice and zest from 1 lemon

3 scallions, chopped fine (green and white parts)

3 slices bacon, fried crisp and finely crumbled

1 Tablespoon extra virgin olive oil

Place the oil and butter in a large heavy skillet over medium low heat. When the butter has melted, add the onions, garlic and carrots. Stir until all the vegetables are well coated. Add the potatoes and stir again until all the potatoes are well coated. Add the dill, salt and pepper to taste. Sauté until the potatoes are almost done, covering the skillet for 3-4 minutes at first. Lay the shrimp on top of the vegetables and cook until just done. Remove from heat and sprinkle lemon juice, scallions and crumbled bacon on top, followed by a little more pepper.

Garnish with lemon zest and extra virgin olive oil.

Serve at tableside with you favorite salad and bread.

Serves 3-4

Poultry Relish

Excellent with roast duck, chicken or turkey

1/2 cup Jerusalem artichokes (sun chokes), peeled, small dice

1/4 cup red onion, small dice

1/4 cup tomato, seeded, small dice

1/4 cup cucumber, peeled and seeded, small dice

1 Tablespoon fresh cilantro, minced

2 Tablespoons extra virgin olive oil

2 teaspoons vinegar

1/4-1/2 teaspoon sugar

1/4-1/2 teaspoon salt

fresh ground black pepper to taste

In a bowl, combine artichokes, onion, tomato, cucumber and cilantro. In a separate bowl, whisk together remaining ingredients. Pour liquid over diced vegetables and toss lightly. Allow flavors to blend 15 minutes.

Serve with roasted poultry or game birds.

Yield: about 1 1/2 cups

Camp three miles N.E. of the Mahar Village
August 15th Wednesday 1804

"I cought a Srimp prosisely of Shape Size & flavour of those about N. Orleans & the lower part of the Mississippi in this Creek which in only the pass or Streight from Beaver Pond to another..."

William Clark

Ruffed Grouse and Dumplings with Cream Gravy

1/2 recipe sourdough bread - frozen bread dough may be substituted. See
   Sourdough Bread recipe on page 43.

2 ruffed grouse, breasted (or substitute chicken breasts)

sifted all-purpose white flour for dredging

2 Tablespoons butter

1 Tablespoon canola

Salt and fresh ground black pepper

1/2 cup water

1 pint heavy cream

After first rising of the bread, shape dough into dumplings (about the size of an egg). Let dumplings rise for one hour. Dredge grouse breast in flour, brown in butter and oil in large dutch oven. Salt and pepper breasts. Add 1/2 cup water to breasts. Bring water to a boil. Reduce heat to low, add dumplings and cover. Simmer with lid on for 45 minutes. Do not lift lid or dumplings will fall. Listen to make sure liquid is still boiling. Remove dumplings and meat to serving plate and keep warm. Add cream to drippings and bring to a boil over medium heat, stirring to loosen drippings. Salt and pepper to taste. Pour over dumplings and meat.

Serves 4

Tuesday August 13th 1805

"on my return to my lodge an indian called me in to his bower and gave me a small morsel of the flesh of an antelope boiled, and a peice of a fresh salmon roasted; both which I eat with a very good relish. this was the first salmon I had seen and perfectly convinced me that we were on the waters of the Pacific Ocean."

Meriwether Lewis

Chinook Salmon Bake

Sauce:

1/4 cup salad dressing

1/4 cup sour cream

1/4 teaspoon cayenne pepper

2 scallions, finely chopped

1 clove garlic, minced

1/2 teaspoon dried dill weed

Main Ingredients:

2-3 pounds Salmon fillets, cut into eight-ounce serving sizes

2 Tablespoons fresh lemon juice

2 Tablespoons butter, melted

1/4 teaspoon seafood seasoning

Garnish:

1/2 cup Cheddar cheese, grated

Seafood seasoning

Combine sauce ingredients in a medium bowl. Set aside. Prepare the fish by squeezing lemon, drizzling butter and sprinkling seafood seasoning on fillets. Grill each side for 3 minutes. Remove from grill and place on broiler pan. Top with sauce, cheese and a dash of seafood seasoning. Broil until cheese melts.

Serves 4

272. *Buffalo and Elk on the Upper Missouri*, watercolor on paper 9 ¾ X 12 ¼

Salt Makers, oil, 24 x 48 inches 1975

Marinades and Sauces

Monday, February 3rd 1806

"late in the evening the four men who had been sent to assist the saltmakers in transporting meat which they had killed to their camp, also returned, and brought with them all the salt which had been made, consisting of about one busshel only. with the means we have of boiling the salt water we find it a very tedious opperation, that of making salt, notwithstanding we keep the kettles boiling day and night. we calculate on three bushels lasting us from hence to our deposits of that article on the Missouri."

Meriwether Lewis

Tarragon and Balsamic Vinegar Marinade

Excellent with Buffalo or Beef

1/4 cup balsamic vinegar

1/4 cup extra virgin olive oil

1/4 cup water

2 Tablespoons Tarragon vinegar

10 Juniper berries, crushed

1/2 teaspoon salt

1/2 teaspoon pepper

1 bay leaf

Combine all ingredients in a self-closing plastic bag. Add meat and marinate for at least 2-3 hours, turning meat at least once. Discard excess marinade. Grill or broil meat according to preference and serve.

Yield: 1 cup marinade

Remarks section of Lewis' weather diary
Feb 11, 1804

"Swans from the N. The sugar maple runs freely."

Meriwether Lewis

Marinated Buffalo Tenderloins with Mango Cucumber Salsa

Marinade

1/8 teaspoon liquid smoke

2 teaspoons fresh ginger, grated

1/4 teaspoon roasted garlic, minced

1 Tablespoon soy sauce

1 Tablespoon ketchup

2 Tablespoons Szechuan sauce

1 shallot, diced fine

1/4 cup hoisin sauce

5 buffalo tenderloins (or beef ribeyes), 1 inch thick

Combine all marinade ingredients in a one-gallon plastic sealable bag, along with buffalo. Seal carefully and place in a pan. Refrigerate for at least 4 hours, turning at least once.

Salsa

1 small jalapeno, seeded and diced

1/2 Tablespoon fresh lemon juice

1/2 Tablespoon lemon zest

2 garlic cloves, minced fine

1 small onion, chopped

1/4 cup cucumber, peeled, seeded and diced

1/2 cup yellow bell pepper, diced

1 mango, peeled, diced

2 large vine ripe tomatoes, seeded and chopped

Wear rubber gloves when handling jalapeno. In a bowl, combine all salsa ingredients and mix thoroughly. Let stand for 10 minutes to allow the flavors to mingle.

Remove steaks from marinade and grill to your preference. Discard excess marinade.

Serve with Salsa

Serves 5

Elk Marinade

14 crushed peppercorns

2 large bay leaves, crushed

1/2 teaspoon dried dill weed

1 teaspoon celery seed

2 teaspoons roasted garlic, minced

1 Tablespoon salt

1/4 cup soy sauce

1/2 cup extra virgin olive oil

3/4 cup Tarragon vinegar

2 cups shallots, minced

3 cups onions, finely chopped

4 elk sirloin steaks (or beef sirloins)

Combine all marinade ingredients in a large saucepan. Bring to a rolling boil, reduce heat and simmer for 5 minutes. Place elk in baking dish with flat bottom. Allow marinade to cool. Pour over elk and refrigerate over night. Remove elk and pour marinade into sauce pan and bring to a boil. Boil for a least 5-10 minutes until marinade is reduced by 1/4. Remove from heat to serve with meat later. Grill elk to your preference.

Yield: 6 cups

Maple Barbecue Sauce

1/2 teaspoon liquid smoke

1 teaspoon celery seed

1 Tablespoon Dijon mustard

2 Tablespoons extra virgin olive oil

2 Tablespoons rice vinegar

1/4 cup shallots, minced fine

1/2 cup maple syrup

1/2 cup chili sauce

Combine all ingredients in small saucepan. Heat to simmer, stirring occasionally. Simmer for 3 to 5 minutes. Remove from heat and coat meat liberally. Grill to your preference, brushing occasionally with remaining sauce.

Yield: 1 1/2 cups

June 10th Sunday 1804

"Camped in a Prarie on the L.S., Capt Lewis and my Self Walked out 3 ms. found the Country roleing open & rich, with plenty of water, great qts of Deer..."

William Clark

Spicy Orange Venison Marinade

1/2 teaspoon salt

1/3 cup extra virgin olive oil

1 teaspoon ground cayenne pepper

2 garlic cloves, minced

1 scallion, minced

1 Tablespoon soy sauce

zest from 1 orange

1 cup fresh orange juice

1 Tablespoon rice vinegar

2 large red bell peppers, seeded and quartered

2 pounds venison tenderloin steaks

Combine all ingredients in a one-gallon plastic sealable bag. Seal carefully and mix thoroughly. Place bag in large baking pan and refrigerate overnight. Grill or broil to your preference. Bring marinade to boiling in sauce pan over medium heat. Boil for at least 5-10 minutes, until marinade is reduced by 1/4. Serve with steak.

Garnish with fresh parsley.

Serves 3-4

Tuesday June 25th 1805

"great quantities of mint also are here. it resemble the pepper mint very much in taste and appearance."

Meriwether Lewis

Cornish Game Hen Marinade

1/8 teaspoon liquid smoke

1 teaspoon lemon zest

1 teaspoon fresh ground black pepper

1 teaspoon dried basil leaves

2 teaspoons roast garlic

1 1/2 Tablespoons extra virgin olive oil

1 1/2 Tablespoons maple syrup

1 1/2 Tablespoons Thai fish sauce (nam pla)

1 1/2 Tablespoons soy sauce

3 Tablespoons fresh ginger, peeled and grated

1/4 cup fresh mint, chopped

1/4 cup fresh cilantro, chopped finely

2 Cornish game hens

Combine all the ingredients (except the game hens) in a blender or food processor. Process at high speed for one minute. Place hens and marinade in a gallon plastic bag. Place bag in a baking pan, seal and refrigerate over night. Place hen on broiler pan and bake at 350 degrees F. for an hour and a half or until done. Baste with marinade every 20 minutes. Remove from oven and allow to set for 15 minutes. Place marinade in a medium sauce pan. Heat to boiling over medium heat. Boil at least 5-10 minutes until marinade is reduced by 1/4. Remove from heat. Serve with hens.

Serves 4

Strip Steak Marinade

1/2 pound of your favorite steak, cut into 1/4-inch thick strips

1 Tablespoon lemon juice

1 Tablespoon lime juice

1 Tablespoon apple cider vinegar

1 teaspoon fresh ground black pepper (or more)

1/2 teaspoon kosher salt

1/2 teaspoon hot pepper sauce (optional)

Place cut steak into a large, sealable plastic bag. In a bowl, whisk together remaining ingredients. Pour liquid into bag containing steak, seal bag and place it into a shallow pan. Marinate for at least 30 minutes, turning once. Steaks may be broiled or grilled; but are best when pan fried in oil. Discard remaining marinade.

Serves 2-3

July 20th , Friday 1804

"Serjt. Pryor & Jo: Fields brought in two Deer this evening— a verry Pleasant Breeze from the N.W. all night— river falling a little, It is wothey of observation to mention that our party has been much healthier on the [Trip] Voyage than parties of the Same Number is in any other Situation"

William Clark

Basic Dry Rub for Meat

This recipe is best with beef, pork or venison;
but is also good with buffalo, elk, turkey or chicken.

1 cup white granulated sugar

1/2 cup kosher salt

4 Tablespoons fresh ground black pepper

1 Tablespoon onion powder

1 Tablespoon garlic powder

1 teaspoon ground cayenne pepper

1/4-1/2 teaspoon liquid smoke (optional)

NOTE: Additional dry spices; such as cumin, sage or basil make wonderful variations in the basic recipe.

Combine all ingredients in a bowl and mix thoroughly. Rub mixture generously into meat and allow it to cure at least 30 minutes. Thicker cuts should be cured longer. Roasts can cure overnight. All rubbed meats should cure in the refrigerator. Meats can be barbecued, grilled, broiled or oven roasted. Store extra rub in a tightly sealed container in the refrigerator. Use within a week.

Yield: about 2 cups

Orange Glaze for Game Birds and Poultry

1/2 cup soy sauce

3 Tablespoons honey

2 scallions, chopped fine

1-2 cloves garlic, minced

1 teaspoon fresh grated ginger

2 teaspoons sesame seeds

juice and zest from 1 orange

Combine all ingredients in a bowl and whisk thoroughly. Allow flavors to blend for 10 minutes. Use as a marinade or brush on during grilling or broiling. Also excellent in stir frys.

Yield: about 1 cup

Sunday March 9th 1806.

"a beautifull duck and one of the most delicious in the world is found in considerable quantities in this neighbourhood during the Autumn and winter. this is the same with that known in the Delliware, Susquehannah, and Potomac by the name of the Canvisback and in James River by that of shell-Drake; in the latter river; however I am informed that they have latterly almost entirely disappeared.   to the epicure of those parts of the union where this duck abounds nothing need be added in praise of the exquiste flavor of this duck. I have frequently eaten of them in several parts of the Union and I think those of the Columbia equally as delicious."

Meriwether Lewis

138

Missouri Mushroom Sauce

1 1/2 teaspoons roasted garlic, minced

4 Tablespoons canola oil

1/4 teaspoon dried basil leaves

1/4 teaspoon ground tarragon

1 pound portabella mushrooms, sliced

1 pound other assorted mushrooms, sliced

2 Tablespoons butter

2 teaspoons Worcestershire sauce

1 teaspoon lemon zest

1 teaspoon lemon juice

In a large bowl, combine garlic, 3 Tablespoons of the oil, basil, and tarragon. Mix well. Add mushrooms and stir until well coated. In a cast iron frying pan over high heat add butter and 1 Tablespoon of oil. Add mushroom mixture and sauté until tender. Remove from heat. Add lemon zest and lemon juice.

Serve over your favorite steak

Yield: about 3 cups

Grilling Sauce for Fish

1/2 cup canola oil

1/2 cup lemon juice

1 teaspoon salt

1/4 teaspoon fresh ground black pepper

1 Tablespoon white granulated sugar

1 teaspoon ground paprika

1 medium onion, sliced

4 halibut or salmon steaks

Combine oil, lemon juice, salt, pepper, sugar, and paprika in sealable plastic bag. Add sliced onion and steaks to bag. Place in shallow dish, seal and refrigerate for two hours. Remove steaks and onions from bag and place in grilling basket. Discard remaining sauce, and grill over medium heat (3 minutes each side).

Serve fish with *Hollandaise Sauce*. See recipe for **Hollandaise Sauce** on page 143.

Serves 4

Thursday August 22ed 1805
"late in the evening I made the men form a bush drag, and with it in about 2 hours they caught 528 very good fish, most of them large trout."

Meriwether Lewis

Wild Chokecherry Glaze for Meat and Poultry

Pan drippings from meat or poultry, about 2-3 Tablespoons

1/4 cup lemon juice

1/2 cup leeks, thinly sliced

1 shallot, minced

1/4 teaspoon salt (or more)

lots of fresh ground black pepper

1/4 cup wild Chokecherry jelly (substitute grape)

1/8-1/4 teaspoon hot pepper sauce (optional)

With skillet over medium low heat, deglaze pan drippings with lemon juice. Add leeks, shallot, salt and pepper. Sauté until leeks are translucent, stirring frequently. Add jelly and hot sauce. Reduce heat and simmer until mixture thickens slightly, stirring often.

Serve over your favorite meat or poultry.

Yield: about 3/4 cup

July 21 Sunday 1805

"emence quantities of Sarvice buries, yellow, red, Purple & black Currents ripe and Superior to any I ever tasted particularly the yellow & purple kind. Choke Cheries are Plenty; Some Goose buries—"

William Clark

Wild Juneberry Glaze for Meat and Poultry

Pan drippings from meat or poultry, about 2-3 Tablespoons

1/4 cup lime juice

1/2 cup leeks, thinly sliced

1 shallot, minced

1/4 teaspoon salt (or more)

lots of fresh ground black pepper

1/4 cup wild Juneberry jelly (substitute blueberry)

With skillet over medium low heat, deglaze pan drippings with lime juice. Add leeks, shallot, salt and pepper. Sauté until leeks are translucent, stirring frequently. Add jelly, reduce heat and simmer until mixture thickens slightly. Stir frequently.

Serve over your favorite meat or poultry.

Yield: about 3/4 cup

Saturday July 20th 1805

"this currant is really a charming fruit and I am confident would be prefered to our markets to any currant now cultivated in the U'States."

Meriwether Lewis

Hollandaise Sauce

2 large egg yolks

2 teaspoons apple cider vinegar

2 Tablespoons heavy cream

1/8 teaspoon hot pepper sauce

1/4 pound (1 stick) butter, ice cold, diced

1/4 teaspoon lime juice

Place egg yolks, vinegar and cream in top half of double boiler (at low boil) and beat until thick. Add pepper sauce and beat. Add diced butter, a small amount at a time (add the next piece after the previous piece has been absorbed). When all the butter has been absorbed, stir in lime juice. Remove from heat, cover bowl until ready to serve.

Serve with grilled meat or fish.

Yield: about 1 cup

Thurday March 13 1806

"The flounder is also an inhabitant of the salt water, we have seen them also on the beach where they have been left by the tide. the Indians eat the latter and esteem it very fine."

Meriwether Lewis

Chipotle Potato Sauce

1 eight-ounce package cream cheese, softened

1 Tablespoon chipotle pepper, minced, with liquid

1 four-ounce can diced green chilies

1 fresh tomato, chopped

2 scallions, 1/4-inch slices

1/2 cup salsa

1/2 cup Cheddar cheese, shredded

seasoned salt

Garnish:

1 scallion, chopped

1/4 cup Cheddar cheese, shredded

In a medium bowl, combine cream cheese with pepper. Add the chilies, tomato, scallions, salsa, cheese, and seasoned salt to taste. Stir well. Serve as topping for baked potatoes or as a tortilla chip dip.

Garnish with more scallions and grated Cheddar.

Yield: about 3 cups of sauce

Undated

"The common wild pittatoe also form another article of food in savage life   this they boil untill the skin leaves the pulp easily which it will do in the course of a few minutes..."

Meriwether Lewis

235. *View of Stone Walls*, watercolor on paper, 9 7/8 X 16 7/8

221. *Rock Formations on the Upper Missouri,*
watercolor on paper, 12 $\frac{1}{2}$ X 7 $\frac{3}{4}$

Desserts

Thursday August 15th 1805

"I found on enquiry of McNeal that we had only about two pounds of flour remaining.   this I directed him to divide into two equal parts and to cook the one half this morning in a kind of pudding with the burries as he had done yesterday and reserve the ballance for the evening. on this new fashioned pudding four of us breakfasted, giving a pretty good allowance also to the Chief who declared it the best thing he had taisted for a long time."

Meriwether Lewis

Two Gun Blackberry Dessert

Filling
1 sixteen and a half ounce can of
  blackberries in light syrup
1 Tablespoon cornstarch
1/2 teaspoon ground nutmeg

Cake
3 cups sifted all-purpose white flour
1/2 teaspoon salt
1 teaspoon baking soda
2 teaspoons baking powder
1 cup granulated white sugar

1 cup of butter, cut in pieces
1 1/2 cups of buttermilk
1 teaspoon vanilla extract
2 eggs, beaten

Topping
1/4 cup butter
3/4 cup granulated white sugar
3/4 cup sifted all-purpose white flour

Preheat oven to 350 degrees F. Grease a 9x13-inch baking pan. Drain berries and reserve liquid. Add 2 Tablespoons of berry juice, cornstarch and nutmeg to a small saucepan. Stir until smooth. Add the rest of reserved liquid and stir. Bring to a boil over medium heat, stirring constantly. Remove from heat. In a large bowl, combine flour, salt, baking soda, baking powder, and sugar together. Cut butter into dry mixture until crumbly. Stir in buttermilk, vanilla and beaten eggs. Spread half the cake mixture into baking pan. Spoon filling over cake mixture. Add remaining cake mixture over filling. Melt butter in a saucepan and blend in sugar and flour until the texture is crumbly. Spoon over cake. Bake 40-45 minutes.

Serve hot with vanilla ice cream.

Yield: 9-12 pieces

The French Voyageurs Wife's Bread Pudding

eight ounces sourdough bread, cut into 1-inch pieces

1 cup whole milk

1 teaspoon vanilla extract

1/2 teaspoon ground cinnamon

1/2 cup granulated white sugar

3 1/2 cups cream, divided

1 cup raisins (optional)

eighteen ounces French white chocolate, chopped, divided

7 large egg yokes

2 large eggs

Toast bread pieces in a 300 degrees F. oven until brown and dry (about 8 minutes). In a large saucepan, over low heat, add milk, vanilla, cinnamon, sugar, 3 cups of the cream and raisins (if desired). Simmer until sugar dissolves, stirring constantly. Add 10 ounces of the chocolate and simmer until melted. Remove from heat and allow mixture to cool slightly. In a separate bowl combine yolks and eggs. Blend until smooth. Add to liquid gradually while stirring constantly. Place bread pieces in a baking dish. Pour half of mixture over bread and press. Allow bread to soak for 10 minutes. Add remaining liquid and cover with foil. Bake for 45 minutes, remove foil and bake an additional 15 minutes until brown. Allow pudding to cool. In a heavy saucepan bring 1/2 cup cream to a simmer, remove from heat and add remaining 8 ounces of chocolate. Stir until smooth.

Serve chocolate sauce over warm pudding.

Serves 5

Louisiana Rice Pudding

2 cups whole milk

1 cup raw white long grain rice

1 cup heavy cream

1/4 cup melted butter

3 eggs, slightly beaten

1 teaspoon vanilla extract

1 cup granulated white sugar

1/2 teaspoon ground cinnamon

1/4 teaspoon salt

1/2 cup walnuts, chopped

1/2 cup raisins

1/4 cup coconut, shredded

Preheat oven to 325 degrees F. In a small saucepan bring milk to a boil, then add rice. Remove from heat and let stand until cool. Combine all ingredients in a large mixing bowl, stirring constantly for 3 minutes. Pour into a shallow baking dish and use a spatula to distribute solid ingredients over bottom of baking dish. Cover top with tin foil and bake for a least 60 minutes until rice is soft and liquids are absorbed. For best results, remove from oven and stir at 20 minute intervals. Remove from heat and allow pudding to rest for at least 15 minutes.

Serve with a little additional heavy cream poured over each portion, and a dash of cinnamon.

Serves 10-12

Juneberry Tart

Pastry for a double crust tart

1 pound juneberries (serviceberries or blueberries)- fresh or frozen

1/2 cup granulated white sugar

2 Tablespoons sifted all-purpose white flour

1/2 teaspoon ground nutmeg

1/4 cup butter

Preheat oven to 400 degrees F. Roll out bottom crust. Lay in dutch oven or on a cookie sheet. Poke crust with fork. In a bowl, toss the berries, sugar and flour. Spread berry mixture on bottom crust. Sprinkle with nutmeg and dot with butter. Roll out top crust and place over berries. Seal edges and slit top. Dot with butter and sprinkle with a little sugar. Bake for 30 minutes, or until crust is golden brown.

Yield: 6 slices

24th August Friday 1804

"...great quantities of a kind of berry resembling a Current except double the Sise and Grows on a bush like a Privey, and the Size of a Damsen deliciously flavoured & makes delitefull Tarts, this froot is now ripe,"

William Clark

Berry Cobbler

1 cup granulated white sugar

3 Tablespoons cornstarch

1/3 cup water

3 cups strawberries, halved

1 cup raspberries

1 1/2 Tablespoons butter

1 teaspoon vanilla extract

In a cold non-reactive sauce pan, combine sugar and cornstarch stirring until cornstarch has no lumps. Add water. Stir until sugar is dissolved. Add berries and cook over medium heat, stirring constantly. When mixture thickens add butter and vanilla and remove from heat.

Topping

2 cups sifted all-purpose white flour

2 Tablespoons granulated white sugar

2 teaspoons baking powder

1/4 cup butter

2 eggs, beaten

1/2 cup cold milk

1/2 teaspoon ground cinnamon

2 teaspoons granulated white sugar

Preheat oven to 350 degrees F. Sift the three dry ingredients together in a large bowl. Cut in butter until dough resembles cornmeal. In a separate bowl combine eggs with milk. Add liquid one tablespoon at a time until dough is just moistened. Pour berry mixture in pie pan. Spoon topping onto berries. Dot top with additional butter. Mix cinnamon and sugar together and sprinkle on topping. Bake for 30 minutes.

Serves 6

Slightly Tart Plum and Blackberry Crumble

Fruit Layer

6-8 large ripe plums, pitted and chopped

2 pints fresh blackberries

Juice from a large lemon

1/4 teaspoon salt

1/3 cup white granulated sugar (double the sugar for a sweeter dessert)

Mix all ingredients together in a bowl and allow flavors to blend for 20-30 minutes.

Crumble Layer

1 cup sifted all-purpose white flour
1/3 cup brown sugar, packed
1/3 cup quick cooking rolled oats
1/4 teaspoon salt
1/2 teaspoon ground cinnamon
dash of allspice
1/2 teaspoon baking powder
1/4 pound (1 stick) butter, softened

Preheat over to 375 degrees F. Mix all dry ingredients in a bowl. Cut in butter until mixture resembles coarse cornmeal. Spread fruit mixture on the bottom of a large baking dish. Sprinkle the dry mixture evenly over the top. Dot top with additional batter if desired . Bake for 45 minutes. Allow dessert to cool about 10 minutes.

Garnish with a dollop of whipped cream and additional plum slices or fresh berries.

Serves 5-6

Serviceberry Pie

4 cups Juneberries (Serviceberries)

1/2 cup water

3/4 cup granulated white sugar

3 Tablespoons tapioca

1 Tablespoon lemon juice

1 teaspoon lemon zest

1 teaspoon vanilla extract

1/4 teaspoon butter flavoring

1/2 teaspoon ground cinnamon

1/4 teaspoon ground nutmeg

pastry for 2 crust 9 inch pie

2 Tablespoons butter

Preheat oven to 375 degrees F. Wash and drain berries thoroughly. Combine water, sugar, tapioca, lemon juice, lemon zest, vanilla, butter flavoring and spices in a medium sauce pan. Bring to a slow boil over medium high heat, stirring constantly. Remove from heat. Press pastry crust into 9-inch pie pan. Prick with fork, pour berries into pie crust, then pour sauce over berries. Dot with butter and top with pie crust. Cut slits in top crust. Sprinkle with sugar and bake for 1 hour.

Yield: 1 pie

July 15 Sunday 1804-
"I Saw Great quantities of Grapes, Plums, or 2 Kinds wild Cherries of 2 Kinds, Hazelnuts, and Goosberries."

William Clark

Missouri River Sand Bars

Crust:

2 1/2 cups sifted white all-purpose
    flour

1 1/2 cups quick cooking rolled oats

1 1/2 cups brown sugar, packed

2 teaspoons baking soda

1/2 teaspoon salt

1 1/2 cups melted butter

1/2 cup pecans

1/4 teaspoon butter flavoring

1/2 teaspoon vanilla extract

Preheat oven to 350 degrees F. In a large bowl combine flour, oatmeal, brown sugar, soda and salt. Stir in butter, pecans, butter flavoring and vanilla extract. Press into 14x18-inch pan and bake for 15 minutes. Remove from heat.

Caramel Sauce:

1 fourteen ounce bag caramels

1 cup cream

1/4 teaspoon butter flavoring

1 teaspoon vanilla extract

Combine sauce ingredients in a medium sauce pan and melt over medium heat stirring constantly. When melted, pour over crust.

Topping:

1 cup chopped pecans

2 milk chocolate bars, grated

Sprinkle bars with topping. Return bars to oven and bake additional 15 minutes.

Yield: 24 bars

Squash Custard Pie

1 1/2 cups winter squash (butternut, acorn or buttercup), cooked and pureed.

3/4 cup granulated white sugar

1/2 teaspoon salt

1/4 teaspoon fresh ground black pepper

1/2 teaspoon ground cinnamon

1/4 teaspoon ground cloves

1 cup cream

2 eggs, beaten

1 teaspoon vanilla extract

1 unbaked 9-inch pie shell

1/4 cup pecans

Preheat oven to 375 degrees F. Combine squash, sugar, salt, pepper, cinnamon, cloves, cream, eggs and vanilla in a medium bowl. Press pecans in bottom of pie shell. Pour custard into pie shell. Bake for 1 hour or until knife inserted in middle comes out clean.

Yield: 1 pie

June 10th Sunday 1804

"I discovered a Plumb which grows on bushes the hight of Hasle [hazel], those plumbs are in great numbers, the bushes beare Verry full, about double the Sise of the wild plumb Called the Osage Plumb & am told they are finely flavoured."

William Clark

Missouri River Breakup

1 package chocolate sandwich cookies (about 1 pound), crushed

1 chocolate and peanut butter candy bar, crushed

1 cup hard toffee candies, crushed

1 cup pecans, chopped

1 carton (1/2 gallon) maple nut ice cream, softened

1 milk chocolate candy bar, shaved and broken

2 white chocolate candy bars, shaved and broken

Crush cookies in bottom of an 8 1/2x11-inch cake pan. Sprinkle candy bar, toffee, and pecans on top of cookies. Pour the softened ice cream on top of candy mixture, top with chocolate bar, then white chocolate. This should resemble the Missouri River during spring break up. Return to freezer until ready to serve.

Yield: 15 squares

30th of April Tuesday 1805

"I walked on Shore to day our interpreter & his Squar followed, in my walk the Squar found & brought me a bush Something like the Current, which She Said bore a delicious froot and that great quantites grew on the Rocky Mountains,"

William Clark

Shortbread

1/4 cup brown sugar, packed

3/4 cup butter

1/4 teaspoon maple flavoring

1/2 teaspoon butter flavoring

1/2 teaspoon vanilla extract

1/4 cup cornstarch

1/8 teaspoon salt

1 1/2 cups sifted all-purpose white flour

Preheat oven to 350 degrees F. In a medium bowl combine sugar, butter and flavorings. Add cornstarch, salt and flour. Stir until well blended. Roll dough out to 1/4 inch thickness. Cut into 40 squares. Place squares on lightly greased cookie sheet. Bake for 10 minutes until golden brown.

Yield: about 40 shortbread

October 29th Tuesday 1805

"Those people are friendly gave us to eate fish Beries, nuts bread of roots & Drid beries and we Call this the friendly Village"

William Clark

Chocolate Summer Squash Cake

1 cup butter, softened

1 3/4 cups granulated white sugar

2 eggs, beaten

1 cup milk

1 teaspoon lemon juice

1/2 cup cocoa

1/2 teaspoon baking powder

1 teaspoon soda

1/2 teaspoon salt

1/2 teaspoon butter flavoring

1 teaspoon vanilla extract

1/2 teaspoon ground cinnamon (optional)

1/4 teaspoon nutmeg (optional)

2 1/2 cups sifted all-purpose white flour

1 white chocolate candy bar, grated

2 cups zucchini, raw, grated

Preheat oven to 350 degrees F. Cream butter and sugar. Add eggs and stir well. In a small bowl combine milk and lemon juice. Sift cocoa, baking powder and salt into butter mixture. Stir well. Add butter flavoring, vanilla, cinnamon and nutmeg to butter mixture. Mix well. Stir milk mixture into butter mixture. Add flour and stir until smooth. Stir in grated chocolate and zucchini. Butter and dust 8 1/2x11-inch pan with powdered cocoa. Pour batter in cake pan and bake in preheated oven for 30 minutes until knife inserted in middle comes out clean. Frost with *Butterscotch Nut Frosting*. See recipe for **Butterscotch Nut Frosting** on page 171.

Yield: 1 cake

Apple Spice Cake

1 cup butter, softened

2 cups granulated white sugar

2 eggs, beaten

1 Tablespoon vanilla extract

1/2 teaspoon butter flavoring

1/2 teaspoon salt

1 teaspoon baking soda

2 teaspoons cinnamon

1/2 teaspoon ground nutmeg

1/4 teaspoon ground black pepper

2 cups sifted all purpose white flour

4 cups thinly sliced apples (cored but not peeled)

Preheat oven to 350 degrees F. In a medium large bowl stir sugar into the softened butter. Add beaten eggs, vanilla and butter flavoring. Sift in salt, soda and spices. Stir well. Sift in flour and stir again. Dough will be very stiff. Add apples and mix until evenly distributed. Pour into buttered and floured 8 1/2x11-inch pan. Bake for 50 minutes (until knife inserted in center comes out clean). Cool and frost with *Creamy White Frosting*. See recipe for **Creamy White Frosting** on page 178.

Yield: 1 cake

August 2nd 1805

"we found a great courants, two kinds of which were red, others yellow deep purple and black, also black goosburies and service buries now ripe and in full perfection, we feasted suptuously on our wild fruit particularly the yellow courant and the deep purple serviceburry which I found to be excellent."

Meriwether Lewis

White Cake

1 cup butter, softened

2 cups granulated white sugar

1/4 cup water (lukewarm)

3/4 cup milk (room temperature)

1 1/2 teaspoons vanilla extract

1 teaspoon soda

1 teaspoon baking powder

1/2 teaspoon salt

2 cups sifted all purpose white flour

5 stiff beaten egg whites (reserve yolks for Lemon Sauce)

Preheat oven to 350 degrees F. Stir sugar into the butter. Add water, milk and vanilla extract and stir. Sift in soda, baking powder, salt and flour. Stir thorougly. Fold in egg whites and pour batter into buttered and floured 8 1/2x11-inch cake pan. Bake for 30 minutes or until knife comes out of center clean. Cool cake. Top with *Lemon Sauce*. See recipe for **Lemon Sauce** on page 176.

Yield: 1 cake

Orderly Book- July 5 1804 - Clark

"I observe great quantities of Summer & fall Grapes, Berries & Wild roases on the banks"

William Clark

Sugar Cookies

1 cup butter, softened

1 cup granulated white sugar

2 eggs, beaten

1 teaspoon vanilla extract

1 teaspoon baking soda

2 teaspoons cream of tartar

3 cups sifted all purpose white flour

Preheat oven to 350 degrees F. Mix butter and sugar. Stir in eggs, vanilla, soda and cream of tartar. Add sifted flour. Chill well (overnight works best). Roll thin and cut in desired shapes. Transfer to cookie sheet and sprinkle with sugar. Bake about 10 minutes or until cookies start to brown. Remove from sheet and set on rack to cool.

Yield: about 2 dozen cookies

October 16th 1805

"after Smokeing with the Indians who had collected to view us we formed a camp at the point near which place I Saw a fiew pieces of Drift wood after we had our camp fixed and fires made, a Chief came from their Camp which was about 1/4 of a mile up the Columbia river at the head of about 200 men Singing and beeting on their drums Stick and keeping time to the musik, they formed a half circle around us and Sung for Some time..."

William Clark

The Lewis Crossing, oil, 24 X 40 inches 1968

260. *Makúie-Póka, Piegan Blackfeet Man,* watercolor on paper, 12 ¼ X 9 ⅞

Assemblage

November 7th 1805
"Great joy in camp we are in View of the Ocian, this great Pacific Octean which we been So long anxious to See. and the roreing or noise made by the waves brakeing on the rockey Shores (as I Suppose) may be heard distictly."

William Clark

Fried Pear Sauce

2 Tablespoons butter

2 pears, cored, peeled and sliced

1/4 teaspoon salt

1/4 teaspoon ground cinnamon

dash of fresh ground black pepper

1/4 cup brown sugar, packed

1/4 teaspoon vanilla extract

1/2 cup heavy cream

Melt the butter in a heavy skillet over medium-low heat. Add pears and sauté, stirring frequently. When pears begin to soften, add salt, cinnamon and pepper. Stir until all pear slices are coated. Sprinkle brown sugar over the top of the pears and stir constantly. When the sugar has mostly caramelized, add 1/4 cup of the heavy cream, stirring constantly for 3-5 minutes. Now add the remaining cream and cook pears for an additional 3-5 minutes. Pears should be completely soft. Carefully transfer sauce to blender (it is HOT!) and pureé until smooth. Pour the pureéd sauce into a serving bowl and allow it to cool slightly.

Serve over your favorite cake or ice cream. Garnish with chopped nuts.

Yield: about 2 cups

Granola Mix

3 cups quick cooking rolled oats

1 cup coconut, shredded

1 cup pecans, chopped

1 Tablespoon toasted sesame seeds

1 cup honey

1/2 cup butter

1/2 cup maple syrup

1 teaspoon vanilla extract

1/2 teaspoon salt

Preheat oven to 350 degrees F. Combine oats, coconut, pecans and sesame seeds in a bowl. In a sauce pan heat honey, butter, syrup, vanilla, and salt until butter is melted. Stir honey mixture into oats mixture. Press in 8 1/2x11-inch cake pan. Bake until brown, (about 20 minutes).

Yield: about 6 cups

July 1st 1804

"G. Drewyer inform that he Saw PueCanns [pecan] Trees on S.S. yesterday great quantities of raspburies an Grapes,..."

William Clark

Campfire Coffee

1 gallon water
1 egg, beaten
1 cup fresh ground coffee
1 cup of water

Bring a gallon of water close to boiling in a large enamel coffee pot. In a small bowl combine egg, coffee and cup of water. Add coffee mixture to boiling water. Bring to a rolling boil. Remove from heat. Grounds will settle to the bottom after coffee cools slightly.

June 25th 1805
"I had a little Coffee for brackfast which was to me a riarity as I had not tasted any Since last winter."

William Clark

Roasted Corn and Artichoke Relish

2 ears of sweet corn, roasted with salt, fresh ground black pepper and olive oil

1 medium onion, small dice

1/4 cup red bell pepper, small dice

1 jalapeno pepper, seeded and diced

6-7 small artichokes hearts, steamed and quartered

2 Tablespoons apple cider vinegar

1/2 cup olive oil

salt and fresh ground black pepper to taste

Cut the kernels from the roasted corn, then combine all ingredients in a bowl. Handle jalapeno pepper with rubber gloves. Cover and chill in refrigerator for 30 minutes.

Serve as a side with your favorite entrée.

Serves 6-8 as a side dish

Thursday August 22ed 1805

"a third speceis were about the size of a nutmeg, and of an irregularly rounded form, something like the smallest of the Jarusolem artichoke, which they also resemble in every other appearance. they had become very hard by being dryed these I also boiled agreebly to the instruction of the Indians and found them very agreeable."

Meriwether Lewis

"Water Million" Pickles

10 cups ripe watermelon, 1 1/2-inch
   cube

8 cups water

1 cup white vinegar

2 teaspoons white granulated sugar

20 sprigs of dill

5 teaspoons salt

1 1/4 teaspoons ground cayenne pepper

5 sterilized wide mouth canning jars

5 sterilized lids

Combine water, vinegar and sugar in a large sauce pan and bring to a boiling over high heat. Reduce heat to low.

Pack each jar as follows: 2 sprigs of dill, 1 teaspoon garlic, 1 teaspoon salt and 1/4 teaspoon cayenne in bottom of jar. Next pack the jar with about 2 cups of cubed watermelons (place a slice of green bell pepper along side of jar). Top with 2 sprigs of dill. Pack the remaining jars. Pour hot water/vinegar mixture into packed jars leaving 1/2 head space. Wipe rims of jars and put sterilized lids on. Hot water bath until peppers lose their vibrant green color (about 10 minutes). Very carefully, remove jars from boiling water and tighten lids. Lids should seal (If they don't, store jar in refrigerator).

Yield: 5 quarts

August the 2nd   1804
"at Sunset 6 chiefs and their warries [warriors] of the Ottos, and Missoures, with a french man by the name of Far fonge, we <Spoke> Shook hands and gave them Some Tobacco & Provisions, they Sent us Water Millions"

William Clark

Butterscotch Nut Frosting

1 cup cream

1/2 cup granulated white sugar

1/2 cup brown sugar, packed

4 egg yolks, beaten

1/2 cup butter

1 teaspoon vanilla extract

1/4 teaspoon butter flavoring

1 cup pecans, chopped

1 milk chocolate bar, grated

Combine cream, sugars, egg yolks and butter in the top of a double boiler. Bring water to boiling over medium heat, stirring constantly. Stir until thick (2 minutes). Remove from heat and cool. Mix in pecans and grated chocolate. Excellent on **Chocolate Summer Squash Cake**, see recipe on page 159.

Yield: about 3 cups

November 1st 1805

"Those people gave me to eate nuts berries & a little dried fish, and Sold me a hat of ther own taste without a brim, and baskets in which they hold their water..."

William Clark

Juneberry Ice

1 cup crushed ice

1/2 cup sparkling water

4 Tablespoons juneberry syrup (chokecherry or blueberry syrup may be
    substituted)

1 teaspoon fresh-squeezed lemon juice

dash of vanilla extract

1 Tablespoon heavy cream

In a blender, combine the ice, water, syrup, lemon and vanilla. Blend until slushy.
Pour into glass and top with cream.

Yield: about 1 1/2 cups

July 17th 1805

"The survice berry differs somewhat from that of the U' States. the
bushes are small sometimes not more than 2 feet high and scarcely ever
exceed 8 and are proportionably small in their stems, growing very
thickly ascosiated in clumps. the fruit is the same form but for the most
part larger more lucious and of so deep a perple that on first sight you
would think them black."

Meriwether Lewis

Roasted Pumpkin Seeds

Seeds from 1 large pumpkin, washed, cleaned and drained (about 2 cups)

1/4 cup canola oil

1/4 teaspoon ground cayenne pepper

1/4 teaspoon ground paprika

1/2 teaspoon seasoned salt

1/2 teaspoon fresh ground pepper

Preheat oven to 350 degrees F. Spread seeds on a baking sheet (with sides) and pour oil over seeds. In a separate small bowl combine spices. Sprinkle over seeds. Bake until seeds are lightly brown (about 20 minutes).

Yield: about 2 cups

14th December Friday 1804

"a fine morning. wind from the S.E. the murcherey Stood at 'O' this morning I went with a party of men down the river 18 miles to hunt Buffalow, Saw two Bulls too pore to kill, the Cows and large gangues haveing left the River, we only killed two Deer & Camped all night with Some expectation of Seeing the Buffalow in the morning, a verry Cold night, Snowed.

William Clark

Winter Sausage

6 pounds ground meat (3 pounds venison and 3 pounds beef)

4 Tablespoons curing salt

2 teaspoons of garlic, minced

3 teaspoons onion powder

3 teaspoons smoke flavored salt

2 teaspoons fresh ground black pepper

2 teaspoons ground paprika

2 teaspoons liquid smoke

2 Tablespoons maple syrup

3 Tablespoons water

coarsely ground pepper corns (optional)

Combine ingredients in large mixing bowl. Cover and refrigerate for about 3 days. Remove from refrigerator. Divide in six parts. Roll each part in a clean flat surface until about 8 inches long. You may roll sausage in pepper corns. Smoke sausage or place sausage on broiler pan. Cover with tin foil and bake in oven at 300 degrees F. for about 1 hour. Meat needs to be well done.

Yield: 6 pounds of sausage

Sauce for Pasta

2 Tablespoons extra virgin olive oil

1/4 cup onions, diced

1/2 cup broccoli, small florets

1 fresh tomato, diced

12 green stuffed olives

eight ounces cream cheese with chives, softened

1 teaspoon dried basil leaves

1 Tablespoon anchovy paste

1/4 teaspoon salt

1/4 teaspoon seafood seasoning

Sauté onions, broccoli, tomato and olives in oil until onion is translucent. Stir in cheese, basil, anchovy paste, salt, and seafood seasoning. Remove from heat and toss with your favorite pasta and serve.

Serve with garlic toast and your favorite salad.

Serves 3-4

Lemon Sauce

1 cup cream

1 cup granulated white sugar

5 egg yolks, blended

1/2 cup butter

juice of 1 lemon (about 1/4 cup)

zest of 1 lemon (about 2 Tablespoons)

In a double boiler, combine cream, sugar, yolks and butter. Stir constantly over boiling water until thick. Add zest and juice and blend well. Remove from heat and let cool slightly. Pour over *White Cake*. See recipe for *White Cake* on page 161.

Yield: about 2 cups

Monday February 24 1806

"I find them best when cooked in Indian stile, which is by roasting a number of them together on a wooden spit without any previous preperation whatever. they are so fat they require no additional sauce, and I think them superior to any fish I ever tasted, even more delicate and lussious than the white fish of the lakes which have heretofore formed my standart of excellence among the fishes. I have heard the fresh anchovey much extolled but I hope I shall be pardoned for beleiving this quite as good."

Meriwether Lewis

Caramel Sauce for Sourdough Sweet Rolls

<u>Sauce:</u>
3 cups brown sugar, packed
1 cup cream
1/2 cup butter
2 teaspoons cinnamon and 1/2 cup sugar combined
butter

While dough is raising, combine sugar, cream and butter over medium heat in saucepan, stirring constantly. Continue stirring until sugar mixture reaches a slow steady boil. Remove from heat and cool. Pour in two 8 1/2x11-inch pans.

<u>Sweet Rolls:</u>
Sourdough for about 2 dozen large rolls
1/4 cup butter; room temperature
2 teaspoons ground cinnamon
1/2 cup granulated white sugar

In small dish combine cinnamon and sugar. Divide dough in 2 parts. Roll dough out to 3/4-inch thickness. Butter generously, sprinkle with cinnamon mixture, roll up and seal dough. Slice dough in 12 equal parts and place in pan. Repeat process with remaining dough. Let raise to desired size. Bake in preheated oven at 350 degrees F for 15-20 minutes until rolls are golden brown.

Yield: 24 rolls

Creamy White Frosting

1 eight-ounce package cream cheese, softened

2 Tablespoons butter, room temperature

1 Tablespoon maple syrup

1/4 teaspoon butter flavoring

2 teaspoons vanilla extract

pinch salt

3 cups powdered sugar, sifted

In a medium bowl combine cheese and butter until blended. Add maple syrup, butter flavoring, vanilla and salt to cream cheese mixture. Stir well. Sift sugar into cheese mixture and blend. Spread on cooled cake.

Yield: about 2 cups frosting

December 23rd 1805

"I also gave a String of wompom to a Chief, and Sent a Small pice of Simimon to a Sick Indian in the Town who had attached himself to me."

William Clark

Maple Taffy

1/2 cup Grade A pure maple syrup

2 Tablespoons butter

6 Tablespoons water

1 1/4 cups white granulated sugar

1/4 cup light corn syrup

1/2 teaspoon butter flavoring

1/2 teaspoon vanilla extract

1/4 teaspoon salt

1/8 teaspoon baking soda

1/2 cup heavy cream

Oil a 11x18-inch pan that is 2 inches deep. Put maple syrup and butter in a large sauce pan. Bring to boil until syrup is reduced to 1/4 cup. Put water, sugar, corn syrup, flavorings, salt and soda in dutch oven. Stir constantly over moderate heat until candy thermometer reaches 235 degrees F. Add cream and stir until candy thermometer reaches 255 degrees. It seems slow at first but temperature rises rapidly at the end. Pour at once into pan. Let cool slightly. With buttered oven proof spatula, start folding in towards center. As soon as taffy is cool enough to handle, divide into four. Pull and twist into ropes. Continue to pull and twist until taffy is golden streaked. Cut into 1 inch chunks.

Yield: about 75 candies

My Favorite Ice Cream

3 cups milk

2 eggs, beaten

2 teaspoons vanilla extract

2/3 cup heavy cream

3/4 cup granulated white sugar

Combine these ingredients and process according to your ice cream maker's instructions. Serve with your favorite toppings.

Yield: 1 quart

Index

Almond and Pear Bread 49
Apple Spice Cake 160
Arikara Autumn Chowder 58
Artichoke Dip 34
Basic Biscuits 51
Basic Dry Rub for Meat 137
Berry Cobbler 152
Berry Spoon Biscuits..53
Blackfoot Pate 29
The Bleu Stag 96
Browned Buffalo Bones Soup 16
Buffalo "Chip" Dip 35
Buffalo Burgers 82
Buffalo Skewers with Peanut Sauce 81
Buffalo Sourdough Pizza 86
Buffalo Strip Sauté 83
Butterscotch Nut Frosting 171
Cajun Buffalo Ribeye Steaks 80
Cajun Catfish Chowder 112
Campfire Coffee 168
Caramel Sauce for Rolls 177
Cheese Biscuits 54
Chinook Salmon Bake 126
Chipotle Potato Sauce...144
Chocolate Summer Squash Cake 159
Clatsop Crab Dip 36
Cole Slaw...69
Corn Dodgers...48
Cornmeal Buns...50
Cornish Game Hen Marinade 135
Cornish Game Hens and Butternut Squash Soup.............................12
Crab and Mushroom Muffins 23
Crab Dip 24
Crab Stew 118
Creamy White Frosting 178

Creole Kale 59

Cucumber Salad 65

Deviled Eggs 32

Discovery Hash 78

Easy Cheesy Salsa Dip 28

Elk and Pork Meatballs 107

Elk Marinade 132

Elk Meatball Soup 11

Elk Stroganoff and Strudels 94

Elk Tortilla Pinwheels 25

Elk with Chokecherry Sauce 104

Favorite Ice Cream 180

The French Voyageurs Wife's Bread Pudding...................................149

Fried Pear Sauce 166

Get Well Soup 18

Grandma's Picnic Potato Salad 60

Grandma's Sourdough Biscuits 45

Granola Mix 167

The Great Portage Baked Beans 66

Grilling Sauce for Fish 140

Harvest Squash Bread 41

Hidatsa Buffalo Stew 90

Hollandaise Sauce 143

Hominy Croquettes 68

Juneberry Ice 172

Juneberry Tart 151

Lakota Fry Bread 44

Lemon Sauce 176

Louisiana Rice Pudding 150

Mandan Buffalo Stew with Winter Squash 77

Mandan Roasted Corn Medley 72

Maple Barbecue Sauce 133

Maple Marinated Buffalo Kabobs 87

Maple Taffy 179

Marinated Buffalo Steaks 79

Marinated Buffalo Tenderloins 131

Marinated Roots and Vegetables 64

Metis Bean Salad 61
Missouri Mushroom Sauce 139
Missouri River Breakup 157
Missouri River Sand Bars..155
One Pot Stew with Cheese Dumplings..................................84
Orange Glaze for Game Birds and Poultry...........................138
Pacific and Columbia Lasagna 113
Pan Blackened Salmon...115
A Peppered Bean Salad 62
Portabella Crab and Cheese Bake..116
Potato Salad...67
Poultry Relish 124
Ribald Manhattan Style Clam Chowder 121
Roast Buffalo..88
Roasted Corn and Artichoke Relish 169
Roasted Pumpkin Seeds 173
Rocky Mountain Vegetable Roast 71
Roots Soup...17
Ruffed Grouse and Dumplings 125
Ruffed Grouse Soup 13
Rye Crackers...52
Saint Louis Buttermilk Cornbread 40
Sauce for Pasta 175
Savory Mustard Venison 98
Sergeant Gass' Pepper Jerky Soup 15
Serviceberry Pie 154
Sharpy's Soup...14
Shortbread 158
Sizzlin' Buffalo Breakfast Sausage 85
Skillet Shrimp and Potatoes 123
Slightly Tart Plum and Blackberry Cobbler 153
Smoked Oyster Stew...117
Smoked Salmon Canapes..27
Smoked Salmon Chowder 122
Sourdough Bread 43
Sourdough Starter...42
Spiced Wild Rice Bread 46

Spicy Buffalo Triangles...26

Spicy Crab Chip Dip...33

Spicy Orange Venison Marinade...134

Spicy Potato Salad...63

Squash Custard Pie...156

Stovetop Pheasant...114

Strip Steak Marinade...136

Stuffed Buffalo Tenderloin...89

Stuffed Mushrooms with Roasted Pine Nuts...31

Stuffed Portabellas...30

Sugar Cookies...162

Sweet and Tangy Meatballs...22

Tarragon and Balsamic Vinegar Marinade...130

Two Gun Blackberry Dessert...148

Venison and Smoked Sausage Soup...10

Venison Breakfast Sausage...106

Venison Chili...102

Venison Jerky...100

Venison Pepper Steak...103

Venison Shepherd's Pie...101

Venison Steak with Cranberry Sauce...105

Venison Stew...99

Venison Swiss Steak...97

Venison with Chokecherry Sauce...108

Virginia Clam Chowder...120

Walleye Chowder...119

Watercress Salad with Vinaigrette Dressing...70

Watermillion Pickles...170

Wedding Waffles...47

White Cake...161

Wild Chokecherry Glaze..141

Wild Juneberry Glaze..142

Wild Raspberry Venison Stew...95

Winter Sausage...174

Lewis & Clark Cookbook Order Blank

QTY		Price
	The Lewis and Clark Cookbook, $19.95 each	$
	ND Residents, add 6% sales tax	$
	Add $3.95 per order for shipping and handling	$
	TOTAL	**$**

Name: _____

Address: _____

City: _____ State: _____ Zip: _____

Telephone: _____ E-mail: _____

Credit Card/Acct. #: _____ Exp. Date: _____

Signature: _____

Send completed order form with payment to:

Whisper'n Waters, Inc.
328 Lunar Lane
Bismarck, ND 58503

VISA, MasterCard, American Express and Discover are welcome.
Phone orders call: 1-888-282-7693 or fax: (701) 223-4259

The Lewis and Clark Cookbook makes a great gift for friends and family.

Gift orders mailed to:

Name: _____

Address: _____

City: _____ State: _____ Zip: _____

Gift Message: _____

Name: _____

Address: _____

City: _____ State: _____ Zip: _____

Gift Message: _____

Name: _____

Address: _____

City: _____ State: _____ Zip: _____

Gift Message: _____

Lewis & Clark Cookbook Order Blank

QTY		Price
	The Lewis and Clark Cookbook, $19.95 each	$
	ND Residents, add 6% sales tax	$
	Add $3.95 per order for shipping and handling	$
	TOTAL	$

Name: _____

Address: _____

City:_____ State:_____ Zip:_____

Telephone: _____ E-mail:_____

Credit Card/Acct. #:_____ Exp. Date:_____

Signature: _____

VISA, MasterCard, American Express and Discover are welcome.

Send completed order form with payment to:

Whisper'n WATERS

Whisper'n Waters, Inc.
328 Lunar Lane
Bismarck, ND 58503

Phone orders call: 1-888-282-7693 or fax: (701) 223-4259

The Lewis and Clark Cookbook makes a great gift for friends and family.

Gift orders mailed to:

Name:_____

Address: _____

City: _____ State:_____ Zip:_____

Gift Message: _____

Name: _____

Address: _____

City: _____ State:_____ Zip:_____

Gift Message: _____

Name: _____

Address: _____

City: _____ State:_____ Zip:_____

Gift Message: _____

Notes:

"Ocian in View! O! the joy."

William Clark

188